RICHARD LONGSETH

D1033388

GREATER YELLOWSTONE

THE NATIONAL PARK AND ADJACENT WILDLANDS
by Rick Reese

Number Six;
Second Edition

MONTANA MAGAZINE
AMERICAN & WORLD
GEOGRAPHIC PUBLISHING
Helena, Montana

ABOUT THE AUTHOR

Rick Reese served as director of the Yellowstone Institute from 1980 to 1984. He was a principal founder of the Greater Yellowstone Coalition and served two terms as president of that organization. He was a park service climbing ranger in Grand Teton National Park for seven seasons and is the author of *Montana Mountain Ranges* in the Montana Geographic Series. Reese is currently a university administrator in Salt Lake City, Utah.

© 1991 American & World Geographic Publishing, all rights reserved

American & World Geographic Publishing
P.O. Box 5630
Helena, Montana 59624. (406) 443-2842

Printed in Hong Kong

Library of Congress Cataloging-in-Publication Data
Reese, Rick.
    Greater Yellowstone : the national park and adjacent wildlands / by Rick Reese. -- 2nd ed.
        p.   cm. -- (Montana geographic series : no. 6)
    Includes bibliographical references (p.   ) and index.
    ISBN 1-56037-004-1
    1. Yellowstone National Park. 2. Yellowstone National Park--Pictorial works. 3. Wilderness areas--Wyoming. 4. Wilderness areas--Montana. 5. Wilderness areas--Idaho. I. Title. II. Series
F722.R37   1991
978.7'52--dc20   91-15964

Right: *Fountain Geyser, Yellowstone National Park.*

Title page: *Side channel of the Snake River in the southern mountains of the Teton Range.*

Front cover: *Minerva Terrace at Mammoth Hot Springs, Yellowstone National Park.* GLENN VAN NIMWEGAN

Back cover, top left: *Penstemon growing amidst sagebrush.* GLENN VAN NIMWEGAN **Bottom left:** *Cottonwood trees in the Lamar River Valley, Yellowstone National Park.* LARRY ULRICH **Right:** *Grizzly bear.*
HENRY H. HOLDSWORTH

HENRY H. HOLDSWORTH

Contents

FOREWORD

by Terry Tempest Williams

An idea was born from the ground up—the Greater Yellowstone Ecosystem; 18 million acres in the Northern Rockies harboring two national parks, six national forests, three national wildlife refuges, other public lands and large enclaves of private land.

Rick Reese, the author of *Greater Yellowstone: The National Park and Adjacent Wildlands*, will tell us the idea was alluded to by Frank Craighead in *Track of the Grizzly*, published in 1979. And that idea was passed along to Reese in the evening discussions he had with John Townsley, superintendent of Yellowstone National Park in the early 1980s when Reese was director of the Yellowstone Institute, and living in the Lamar Valley with his wife and two children.

But what Rick Reese won't tell you is that he corralled the concept, beat the drums, spoke the words, and made it happen. The Greater Yellowstone Ecosystem as an idea has not only entered our mind, but also our language, initiating social change within the natural resource community through public perception. An individual with a vision restored natural boundaries—not ours, but the land's.

The future of the American West, our wildlands and our communities, will turn on the long view of its residents. Rick Reese has always climbed mountains. He grew up in Utah with the Wasatch Range as the backdrop for his childhood. At 14 he was intimate with granite, at 16, he and two young friends climbed Mount Rainier; at 17, he climbed the Grand Teton. These are impressionable years that burn deeply in one's soul.

Perhaps the wide view Reese saw as a young man from the crown of the Tetons translated years later into his dream of the Greater Yellowstone. We are the beneficiaries of this climber's life where a poetics of place was transformed into a politics of place.

It's a lesson for all of us. Big thoughts are born in big country. If we want to preserve the human imagination, we must preserve the wildlands that inspire us.

The Greater Yellowstone Ecosystem is our nation's medicine bundle. It must remain intact and whole. Let us send up our prayers, remembering the grizzly, remembering the wolf, remembering the white wings of trumpeter swans. May we never forget each pilgrimage is holy.

Specimen Ridge looking toward Slough Creek at sunset.

GEORGE WUERTHNER

TOM MURPHY

Lower Falls of the Yellowstone River.

PREFACE

The concept of a Greater Yellowstone first came to my attention early in the summer of 1981 shortly after our family arrived in Yellowstone National Park, where I had been appointed director of the Yellowstone Institute. We moved to Mammoth early in June and were assigned to live in the enormous stone home situated between the Albright Visitor Center and the residence of the park superintendent. That historic seven-bedroom, three-story home once was occupied by the military commanders of old Fort Yellowstone, years before there was a National Park Service.

But in looking back, what was important about that home was that it was next door to the home of John Townsley, then superintendent of Yellowstone National Park. John had grown up in a park service family and at an early age learned natural history and conservation at the field school in Yosemite National Park, where his father was chief ranger. His children were grown, his wife spent much of her time in California, and John lived alone in Yellowstone most of the year. He was a

crusty, sometimes brusque and, I think, lonely man whose abrupt manner did not endear him to some of his park service employees.

During that first summer in Mammoth, I had the opportunity to spend some evenings visiting with our new neighbor and came to know this man, John Townsley.

That same summer, Secretary of the Interior James Watt and his friends in Washington had come up with an unprecedented scheme to open 92,000 acres of the Washakie Wilderness to oil and gas exploration and development. The Washakie abuts Yellowstone National Park for a number of miles along the east park boundary.

Townsley appeared at a hearing on the Washakie oil and gas proposal in mid-June, 1981 and, speaking in his official capacity as superintendent of Yellowstone National Park, he vigorously criticized the proposal to open the Washakie to development. Within a few days he heard from his displeased superiors in Washington, who told him in no uncertain terms that what happened on federal lands outside Yellowstone National Park was none

of his business, that he should keep his nose out of matters beyond Yellowstone's boundaries, and that if he didn't, he would be replaced.

Shortly after John returned to Yellowstone from the Washakie hearing and after his subsequent roasting, I visited with him on the back steps of his home. I'll never forget our conversation that June night in 1981. He told me that to treat Yellowstone Park as a box on a map, with no regard for threats to the park from neighboring national forest lands, was absurd. He said that the biological and geological wonders of Yellowstone were threatened by activities on adjacent lands; that a new recognition of the interrelatedness of these lands was desperately needed; and that Yellowstone Park itself was but one portion of a much larger region whose lands were inextricably linked. The American people, he said, must be educated about these interrelationships and must begin to think in terms of a "Greater Yellowstone Ecosystem."

Through that summer and fall and into the long Montana winter of 1981-1982, I

The swift metamorphosis and the onward march of civilization, sweeping ever eastward, and transforming and taming our wilderness, fills us with a strange regret, and we rejoice that parts of that wilderness will yet remain to us unchanged. Amid our glorious mountains, snowcrowned and towering to the clouds, sheltering in their rocky embrace so many beautiful parks, broad basins and rich valleys, we can yet recall the charm of the wilderness we once knew.

WILLIAMS S. BRACKETT
PARK COUNTY, MONTANA
1900

read a great deal about Yellowstone, and in the spring began work on a manuscript that elaborated on the concept of a Greater Yellowstone Ecosystem, documented the threats to the ecosystem's integrity and called for coordinated, ecosystem-wide management.

By the summer of 1982 I was beginning to ask the right questions and benefitted enormously from extensive conversations with the zoologists, botanists, geologists, biologists and other scientists who streamed through the Yellowstone Institute.

It was also during 1982 that early discussions began about forming a regional conservation organization dedicated to protection of the Greater Yellowstone region. In mid-January of that year I met with Ralph Maughan in Bozeman to discuss the creation of what we then called the "Greater Yellowstone Alliance." Though nothing came immediately out of that meeting, we started thinking about an organization. In October of that year I presented a slide documentary in Bozeman at the "Greater Yellowstone Environmental Symposium" sponsored by the Madison-Gallatin Alliance, a new organization that focused its attention on resource management in the Gallatin and Madison river drainages.

The next year, I completed my manuscript, and production started on the first edition of this book. In May, we convened a group of individuals at the Teton Science School in Jackson Hole for the purpose of organizing the Greater Yellowstone Coalition. I served as the first president of that fledgling organization that today has thousands of individual members, 90 organizational members, a staff of 13 and an annual budget of more than half a million dollars.

Early in 1984, *Greater Yellowstone: The National Park and Adjacent Wildlands* was published. John Townsley did not live to see the book or the

creation of the Greater Yellowstone Coalition. He died of cancer in September 1982, never knowing that the seeds he planted on the steps of his back porch that summer evening in 1981 would bear such fruit.

To this day I do not know where John Townsley came up with the term "Greater Yellowstone Ecosystem." It's likely that he found it in Frank Craighead's *Track of the Grizzly*, an engaging book about the Craighead brothers' bear research in Yellowstone published in 1979. Craighead had used the term "Greater Yellowstone Ecosystem" at least once in his book and had made several other references to the "Yellowstone Ecosystem," which he equated with the range of the Yellowstone grizzly population, an area approximately twice the size of Yellowstone National Park itself. By this measure the ecosystem's extent would be about 4.5 million acres.

But, *Track of the Grizzly* told us little about the concept of a Greater Yellowstone Ecosystem. What is an ecosystem? Are there criteria other than bear range to define the boundaries of a Greater Yellowstone? What are our management goals and how will they be achieved? Are there forces of change underway that individually and/ or cumulatively may threaten the integrity of the ecosystem (however defined), and if so, what are they? Are we able to cope with such forces? Should we? What organizations or individuals are able to answer these questions and act on them? And what are the long-term objectives that will guide them?

There was clearly much more that needed to be said about the "Greater Yellowstone Ecosystem." The publication of *Greater Yellowstone: The National Park and Adjacent Wildlands* represented a modest first step at approaching these questions. In it, I set forth five themes to be explored and

Aspens in Yellowstone National Park.

PAT O'HARA

Prints in the snow chronicle a hawk's successful mouse hunt.

TOM MURPHY

developed, which are worth repeating here: 1) Yellowstone National Park is a very special and, in some respects, a unique place; 2) the park is not an island, but rather exists in an ecological context that we call the Greater Yellowstone Ecosystem; 3) the entire Greater Yellowstone Ecosystem is an extraordinary national treasure existing as the largest, essentially-intact ecosystem remaining in the temperate zones of the earth; 4) most resource management decisions in the Greater Yellowstone Ecosystem are made in a fragmented manner that does not recognize the area as a single ecological unit, but rather views it as more than two dozen separate political and administrative entities; 5) the Greater Yellowstone Ecosystem is imperiled by activities and developments that pose imminent threats to its environmental integrity.

For many today, these propositions may seem self-evident, but in 1983 they were extremely controversial. At that time, no one had yet developed the concept of a Greater Yellowstone Ecosystem, attempted to define the boundaries of such an entity, applied it to the need for integrated, coordinated management, and discussed it in terms of the astounding array of "development" activities that threatened to disrupt it. Federal land managers refused to use the term Greater Yellowstone Ecosystem, or to even acknowledge that such an entity existed. Commodity producers viewed the ecosystem concept as a scheme to expand the boundaries of Yellowstone, and some scientists questioned the legitimacy of a layman/author applying a term as slippery as "ecosystem" to the Greater Yellowstone region.

But these themes fell on fertile fields, and the acceleration of understanding and acceptance of the notion of a threatened Greater Yellowstone Ecosystem was astounding. More significantly, that understanding led quickly to new management directions and policies.

Since the publication of the first edition of this book in 1984, more than 170 articles and books (that I am aware of) dealing with the Greater Yellowstone Ecosystem have appeared; TV specials have run on every major network; more than a dozen conferences have been held; politicians of both parties have spoken at length about the Greater Yellowstone Ecosystem as have park superintendents, National Forest supervisors and cabinet-level bureaucrats. In 1985, William Penn Mott, then director of the National Park Service, gave a speech in which he repeated almost verbatim the five themes outlined in this book; later that same year Congress held oversight hearings on the Greater Yellowstone Ecosystem and the Congres-sional Research Service issued a study concluding that the Greater Yellowstone Ecosystem was an "identifiable landform," that numerous activities threatened to disrupt it, and that management of the ecosystem was uncoordinated.

In 1987 the Regional Office of the U.S. Forest Service undertook a project to "aggregate" all national park and national forest management plans in the entire Greater Yellowstone area. In 1990 a federal interagency organization calling itself the Greater Yellowstone Coordinating Committee issued a draft of its *Vision for the Future: A Framework for Coordination in the Greater Yellowstone Area*, calling for coordinated management of all federal lands in the region. In 1987, Clark and Zaunbrecher, writing in the *Renewable Resources Journal*, called the application of the ecosystem label to the Greater Yellowstone region a "major innovation in natural resources policy." In the summer of 1989, President George Bush spoke of "Greater Yellowstone" in a speech at the Teton Science School and referred to it as "one of the last intact ecosystems." A basic shift in our thinking about Yellowstone had occurred.

There have been some remarkable changes in Yellowstone and in the way we think about Yellowstone in the seven years since the first edition of this book. A great deal of scientific effort has been devoted to developing a clearer understanding of what an ecosystem is and to redefining the general boundaries of the Greater Yellowstone Ecosystem; the notion of "ecosystem management" has been introduced, debated and to some extent implemented; the Greater Yellowstone Coalition has blossomed into one of western America's most effective conservation organizations; Alston Chase's highly controversial book, *Playing God in Yellowstone*, was published; and massive fires (covered in a new section in this edition by George Wuerthner) burned across the ecosystem during the dry, windy summer of 1988. These changes combined to make the 1980s truly watershed years for the Greater Yellowstone Ecosystem.

WHAT IS AN ECOSYSTEM?

One dictionary defines "ecosystem" as a "complex of ecological community and environment forming a functioning whole in nature." But how we define any particular ecosystem depends upon the components taken into account and the time period considered. An ecosystem in its simplest form is an area that functions as a self-contained natural unit. By this definition it could be something as small as an anthill or as large as the

Moose Basin, Grand Teton National Park.

PAT O'HARA

planet. In the case of Yellowstone, we could, as I suggested in 1984, define the Greater Yellowstone Ecosystem as that area containing all the elements required to perpetuate all the indigenous species of the area. Or we could define it in terms of vegetation types or according to any other natural component. The Greater Yellowstone Coalition in its 1990 draft Profile document referred to the Greater Yellowstone *Ecosystem* as "one of the last wildlands where natural processes and disturbances of large magnitude are allowed to operate with minimal human manipulation."

But no matter how you define the term "ecosystem," the concept's importance lies in its recognition that lines on a map are irrelevant to the web of nature within a self-contained natural unit requiring little or no human input to function. This is not difficult to understand, but in 1984, and to a lesser extent today, understanding it requires a new way of looking at things. And I would maintain now, as I did then, that ecosystems are not merely fictional models useful as instructional devices. It is possible to delineate general boundaries of ecosystems, given the qualification that those boundaries be regarded more as permeable membranes than as rigidly fixed. And further, those boundaries are not totally arbitrary, given a set of agreed upon components.

ECOSYSTEM BOUNDARIES

In the case of the Greater Yellowstone Ecosystem a variety of different components (wildlife, geological features, soils, vegetation and altitude)

Right: *Coyote and elk herd.*

Facing page: *Brown-headed cowbird passengers for an elk cow.*

suggest roughly the same ecosystem boundaries. This is not difficult to understand, given the determining influence that each of these components has on the others—geology affects elevation and soils; soils affect vegetation; vegetation affects wildlife and so on. This is more than a fictional model—it defines an area in which elevation, hydrology, flora, fauna and human use patterns are distinctly different from surrounding areas.

The maps that appeared in the first edition of the book depicted a Greater Yellowstone Ecosystem that encompassed 8 to 10 million acres. At the time, such a proposition seemed bold given the resistance of federal agencies and commodity producers to the delineation of a Greater Yellowstone Ecosystem. I noted at the time that even though the potential natural vegetation component suggested an ecosystem that stretched for miles to the south and southeast (to beyond a line drawn roughly from Afton to Lander) these lands

were omitted because of their distance from the ecosystem's center. I said then that this arbitrary judgment was based on editorial, not ecological considerations, and concluded that "a case could certainly be made for including [the additional lands]."

In retrospect, it is clear that I was too conservative. Those lands to the south and southeast and others should have been included in the ecosystem boundaries. Today, even the U.S. Forest Service in the Greater Yellowstone Coordinating Committee *Aggregation* document defines Greater Yellowstone as an area of more than 18 million acres and describes it as "the continuous mountainous region in and around Yellowstone National Park." By contrast, Yellowstone Park itself is a mere 2.2 million acres.

But while it is useful to delineate some general and permeable boundaries to our ecosystem, remember that the boundaries themselves

TOM MURPHY

TOM MURPHY

NEAL & MARY JANE MISHLER

In late November, bighorn rams fight for dominance of their herd.

are less important than how the components of the system relate to one another.

ECOSYSTEM MANAGEMENT

In 1984 I noted that management of the Greater Yellowstone Ecosystem was fragmented between nearly two dozen political subdivisions including two national parks, seven national forests, three National Wildlife Refuges, three states and a maze of counties, local, state and federal agencies. I called for integrated management based on area-wide considerations and even went so far as to suggest consideration of bringing all federal lands in the region under the management of one entity. Two and a half years later the Congressional Research Service issued a lengthy report noting that "existing administrative boundaries and organizations hamper comprehensive, coordinated understanding and management" and concluding that there was little likelihood of coordinated management in the Greater Yellowstone Ecosystem under current administrative structures.

Since that time, it has become increasingly apparent that this management fragmentation and its corresponding failure to factor cumulative and ecosystem-wide considerations into management decisions is, in itself, a serious threat to preserving the ecological integrity of the Greater Yellowstone.

In recent years the term "ecosystem management" has been used to describe the integrated management that is so crucial to the future of Greater Yellowstone. During that time I have learned (through the writings of Dr. Tim Clark and others) that coordinated management and "ecosystem management" are not the same thing. In ecosystem management, the entire ecosystem is viewed and treated as one dynamic, interactive unit and management seeks not merely to protect individual elements, but also seeks to maintain the linkages between individual elements. Traditional management practices, on the other hand, typically focus on managing or extracting a specific resource without necessarily considering impacts on other ecosystem components. Traditional management may be highly coordinated, yet still ignore the principles of ecosystem management.

Ecosystem management values all resources within the system, whether or not they have economic or even aesthetic value. The goal is not simply to benefit humans but rather to preserve and benefit all species.

The term "ecosystem management" can be ambiguous and frequently is misunderstood. To some, it is synonymous with "locking up" resources and has been attacked by logging, mining and other commodity interests. In fact, commodity production, properly pursued, can be very compatible with ecosystem management.

In the 1990 draft of its *Vision* document, the Greater Yellowstone Coordinating Committee speaks of both coordinated management and ecosystem management, sometimes interchangeably. Noting that the document represents "new ways of doing business...the central element of shift is toward ecosystem management," the committee goes on to declare that "No place on earth is there a more fitting site to pioneer ecosystem management" [than in Greater Yellowstone]. Elsewhere in *Vision* the authors say that "...the Forest Service and Park Service will coordinate and communicate to an extent not previously experienced in the long history of the two agencies." It is yet unclear whether the federal agencies are looking beyond simply coordinating management to true ecosystem management as defined above.

THE NATURAL REGULATION CONTROVERSY

A great political controversy has erupted in the past few years over some mistaken assumptions about a phenomenon that has come to be known as "natural regulation."

In a landmark 1963 report, *Wildlife Management in the National Parks*, the preeminent naturalist A. Starker Leopold and a panel of other scientists called for managing America's natural parks "to preserve to the greatest extent possible the biotic assemblages that existed, or would have evolved, without the advent of European settlement." The Leopold report called for allowing nature, to the greatest possible extent, to take its course without the interference of humans, and to protect all the necessary ingredients for a smooth-functioning, self-regulating ecosystem.

But people have interfered, and still do so and natural regulation must therefore be regarded as an ideal, an objective not absolutely attainable. Natural regulation also recognizes that past biological disruptions incurred by humans should be undone to the extent possible in an attempt to solve the resulting problems.

Natural regulation does not mean "hands off" in every situation; neither does it mean slavish and inflexible adherence to the ideal. In the first edition of this book I expressed the realization that although "the overwhelming majority of Yellowstone Park is still wild, the Park is not pristine" and went on to note that "The policy of non-interference should not be confused with the policy of no management." I also said that "man has so altered natural systems that he must re-interfere to try to restore them. It remains to be seen if this can ever be fully achieved..."

Natural regulation as practiced by Yellow-

Stay on this good fire-mountain and spend the night among the stars. Watch their glorious bloom until the dawn, and get one more baptism of light. Then, with fresh heart, go down to your work, and whatever your fate, under whatever ignorance or knowledge you may afterward chance to suffer, you will remember these fine, wild views, and look back with joy to your wanderings in the blessed old Yellowstone Wonderland.

JOHN MUIR, 1898

stone Park biologists, for example, would likely seek restoration of a lost species or process rather than abiding such a loss, but at the same time would probably favor the minimum amount of restoration required to achieve a maximal recovery of nature. Interference and remediation are not necessarily disclaimed, but the less the better.

Given the controversy this idea has spawned in the last five years, it is important to understand that natural regulation is an ideal and that no scientist I know believes it is perfectly achievable in all of Greater Yellowstone.

In 1986 Alston Chase wrote a book entitled *Playing God in Yellowstone: The Destruction of America's First National Park*. Chase, a former philosophy professor who had come west some years earlier, took up residence south of Livingston, Montana in the early 1980s.

Chase's book caused an immediate controversy over the question of natural regulation. He alleged that beginning sometime in the 1960s a gigantic conspiracy emerged between environmentalists and National Park Service officials in Yellowstone National Park. The purpose of the conspiracy was to implement natural regulation, a policy that, according to Chase, subsequently led to grave environmental disasters in Yellowstone National Park.

At the hands of Chase, natural regulation was alleged to be a misguided and inflexible ideology slavishly adhered to by the National Park Service in Yellowstone. If fact, however, responsible adherents of natural regulation never had claimed for it what Chase said they claimed. His target was natural regulation as he defined it, and indeed it was an easy target. He selectively quoted the 1963 Leopold report, failing to mention that it clearly stated that hands-off management would not work and that "reluctance to undertake biotic management can

never lead to a realistic presentation of primitive America.…"

In place of natural regulation, Chase called for hands-on "scientific" management for Yellowstone, but never told his readers what that meant. He equated "ecosystem management" and "natural regulation," failing to understand the application of either. Chase's book was a classic example of misunderstanding the meaning and intent of natural regulation as practiced by the National Park Service.

THE GREATER YELLOWSTONE COALITION

When the Greater Yellowstone Coalition (GYC) was created in 1983, no one could have foreseen how quickly and effectively it would both promote the ecosystem concept and organize grass roots protection of the Greater Yellowstone.

The GYC was an immediate success, but by late 1985 was experiencing severe growing pains. An extraordinary effort by board members Maryanne Mott, Bill Bryan and others, and gritty determination by a small, dedicated staff led by Louisa Wilcox, brought the organization into the autumn of 1986 staffed by a new executive director, Ed Lewis, and armed with rekindled enthusiasm for the task at hand. From that time forward, the GYC has enjoyed remarkable success in its program of resource protection, public education and organizational development. This coalition of several thousand individuals and 90 organizations has given wings to an idea, developing it into a genuine public movement.

FUTURE DIRECTIONS

When we think in terms of ecosystems, we become more aware of interdependence in a region. In the case of the Greater Yellowstone Ecosystem, our cognizance of region-wide interdependence has dramatically increased our awareness of the scope and gravity of what I have called "threats to the ecological integrity" of the Greater Yellowstone. Until recently, the American public did not think of mining in the Beartooth Mountains, or oil and gas drilling in the Bridger-Teton National Forest, or massive timber clear cutting on the Targhee National Forest as threats to Yellowstone National Park, because these activities took place outside the park boundary—as if a line on a map could somehow protect Yellowstone from adverse external impacts.

That is why I have devoted so much of this book to examining these threats. And it is one reason I disagree so sharply with someone like Alston Chase, who wants to overlook the massive development of extractive resource projects on the lands surrounding Yellowstone Park and focus instead on the allegedly damaging results of a perceived conspiracy to manage the park under an "ideology" of misstated natural regulation.

Our ecosystem-wide perspective also helps us understand the cumulative effect of threats, any one of which, taken by itself, may have no apparent negative impacts. But when viewed together with other projects elsewhere in the ecosystem can portend dramatic consequences.

This is not to say that no extractive industries should operate in this region—only that their cumulative region-wide impact on the ecosystem should be taken into account.

Multiple use of our national forests does not mean every conceivable use on every acre of every

Great gray owl.
TOM MURPHY

national forest. It means utilizing national forests for a variety of purposes and recognizing that some uses are not appropriate on some portions of some forests. Deciding how to allocate such uses is a challenging and extremely controversial issue in the Greater Yellowstone Ecosystem.

What is the highest and best use of the lands of Greater Yellowstone? What priorities should guide us in making this judgment? *Sustainability* must be the central consideration in answering these questions. If we can agree that Greater Yellowstone is an extraordinary national treasure, that it is in some respects even unique, and that it is one of the largest, essentially-intact ecosystems remaining in the temperate zone of the earth, then in my view we should protect it so generations to come may enjoy and value it as we do. Fortunately, the same policies that will preserve Greater Yellowstone will also yield the greatest long-term economic return to the region. If we play our cards wisely, we can have both preservation and maximum long-term, sustainable economic return.

Tourism and recreation are by far the largest sources of employment on federal lands in the Greater Yellowstone region. Properly managed, tourism is largely non-consumptive and therefore sustainable. If we can preserve what visitors are willing to spend hundreds of millions of dollars every year to see and experience, we will preserve the source of our income forever. This is what the Greater Yellowstone Coalition is talking about in their 1991 *Environmental Profile*, by Glick, Carr and Ekey, when they call for "living off the interest of the landscape rather than drawing from its capital assets."

And what is it that brings visitors back to the Greater Yellowstone region year after year, decade after decade? It is wild land—natural, vast, and intact—and its concomitants: wildlife, open space, natural marvels, clean air and water and, perhaps most important of all, opportunities for spiritual renewal and reflection. Our mission is to husband and conserve all of this. And to conserve not only the biological and geological treasures of Greater Yellowstone for their own sakes, but in so doing to preserve what Olaus Murie called our "sources of inspiration."

This is not to say that tourism should be the exclusive economic activity here—but it should take precedence over other activities that will diminish the area's attraction to visitors. There are certainly instances in which resource extraction and tourism are compatible, but in many other instances they are not; choices between competing values will have to be made.

In 1886, as the U.S. House of Representatives argued over a proposed railroad through Yellowstone National Park, Rep. William McAdoo noted that "a land famine is approaching" and that the Yellowstone region should be preserved, if for no other reason, because "The glory of this territory is its sublime solitude. Civilization is becoming so universal that man can only see nature in her majesty and primal glory in these as yet virgin regions." In the century since McAdoo uttered these words, America's "yet virgin regions" have dwindled to a few islands. In the entire lower 48 states, Greater Yellowstone now stands as perhaps the largest least disturbed of all these, and McAdoo's words ring truer than ever.

—*Rick Reese*
February 1991

The Absaroka Range north of Yellowstone National Park, viewed from Mount Washburn inside it. JEFF VANUGA

PREFACE

In the pages that follow I have attempted to develop five themes: (1) Yellowstone National Park is a very special and, in some respects, a unique place; (2) the national park itself is not an island, but rather exists in an ecological context that we call the Greater Yellowstone area; (3) the entire Greater Yellowstone Ecosystem is an extraordinary national treasure existing as the largest essentially-intact ecosystem remaining in the temperate zones of the earth; (4) most resource management decisions in the Greater Yellowstone Ecosystem are made in a fragmented manner, which does not recognize the area as a single ecological unit, but rather views it as more than two dozen separate political and administrative entities; (5) and that the Greater Yellowstone Ecosystem is imperiled by activities and developments that pose imminent threats to its environmental integrity.

I have not directly approached the question of how much development is desirable on the lands of Greater Yellowstone, but my personal bias clearly favors maintaining in a natural condition as much of the entire eco-system as we possibly can. But no matter how we as individuals or as a nation answer the question of what is an acceptable degree of development for Greater Yellowstone, we must recognize that there will be trade-offs. If we opt to give up more of our wild lands in Greater Yellowstone, we should do it with the full recognition of what will be gained and what will be lost. We should acknowledge that the impacts at one point in the ecosystem also will be felt elsewhere in the area and in ways we can't always predict. We must also proceed in a manner that allows us to openly assess the trade-offs, on a local as well as on an ecosystem-wide scale. For most of three centuries, American society has operated on the assumption that the earth has been endowed with natural resources to serve only humans, who consume without regard for other living creatures or even for the people of future generations. That attitude often has led us to focus only on the gains to be realized from natural resource exploitation with no real understanding of the corresponding losses. Frequently, costs in the form of degraded land became apparent only after it was too late. Today in the face of the stark reality that we are finally down to the very last remnants of wild land in our country, a new attitude is more appropriate; an attitude that recognizes that our Creator, in providing the earth, gave us a unique gift, an island of habitability in a universe of hostile space, a planet so delicate, so irreplaceable and so fundamental to the survival of the only life we know, that it merits our stringent stewardship and nurturing. In this view conservation, not consumption, should be the driving force of society, maintaining to the highest possible degree the natural face of our fragile planet. By this reckoning, drilling and mining the wilderness, logging the shrinking habitat of threatened species, poisoning our waterways, destroying the great bear and diminishing our park lands have no place. We are not yet that poor as a nation.

—*Rick Reese*
November 1983

INTRODUCTION

There is a place high astride the Continental Divide in the northern Rocky Mountains of western America where within a few miles of one another the first trickles of the Snake, the Yellowstone and the Green rivers are born. From here everything goes down: to the Columbia, to the Missouri, to the Colorado and on to the sea. During the exploration of the west, this place, where present-day Montana, Idaho and Wyoming converge, was the last major piece to be fitted into the giant puzzle of American geography.

By the time a definitive exploration of the Yellowstone region finally was accomplished in 1871, the remainder of the west was largely settled: the Mormons had been in Utah for more than 20 years, the valleys of the west were being farmed and ranched, John Wesley Powell had explored and mapped the Grand Canyon and the Colorado River, the California gold rush had come and gone, and

STEVEN FULLER

the fires of the Civil War had been cold for half a decade. A few white men had penetrated the region; one, John Colter of the Lewis and Clark expedition, had walked alone through here in search of furs as early as 1807. Intermittently for the next 60 years an occasional trapper, prospector or explorer would make his way into what mountain men and explorers loosely called The Yellowstone, and a few would even chronicle it as did Osborne Russell, who wrote so eloquently of the area in the 1830s. However, by the latter third of the 19th century, the region of the upper Yellowstone was still essentially terra incognita.

In 1860 an able expedition of the Corps of Topographic Engineers under the leadership of Captain William F. Raynolds made an attempt at an organized exploration of the Yellowstone region, but the expedition failed to penetrate even the outer reaches of the area that today comprises Yellowstone National Park. It was another nine years before three curious adventurers, David E. Folsom, Charles W. Cook and William Peterson, set out in the autumn from near Helena in Montana Territory to conduct their own exploration. Only upon the return of these three to civilization after nearly a month of plying Yellowstone's inner recesses did a comprehensive understanding of the area began to emerge.

Armed with the invaluable information of the Cook-Folsom-Peterson expedition and encouraged by their findings and success, another expedition to Yellowstone under the leadership of Henry D. Washburn, Surveyor General of Montana Territory, was launched from Helena in 1870. This group, consisting of a military escort and 19 people including several of considerable wealth and political influence, covered much of the ground that Cook, Folsom and Peterson had seen the year before. In addition, Washburn and his party traveled deep into the southeast portion of Yellowstone nearly circumscribing Yellowstone Lake. Upon their return, various members of the expedition wrote articles about the upper Yellowstone and attracted considerable national attention to the wonders they had seen. One of their number, Nathaniel P. Langford, went forth to deliver a series of lectures including one in January 1871 in Washington, D.C. Dr. Ferdinand V. Hayden, head of the U.S. Geological Survey of the Territories, was in the audience. Out of this contact between Langford and Hayden were sown the seeds of the famous Hayden Survey of Yellowstone in 1871, the most productive, definitive and elaborate of all the Yellowstone expeditions.

Hayden assembled a large and talented scientific party of geologists, zoologists, botanists and a variety of others including photographer William H. Jackson and artist Thomas Moran. His highly successful expedition gathered hundreds of specimens in addition to producing a wealth of notes, photographs and artistic sketches, and confirmed the wonders of Yellowstone—up to that time largely unverified.

In Washington, Hayden set about compiling his findings in an official report that joined others in urging Congress to set aside the Yellowstone region as America's first national park. That was accomplished just a few short months later when, in March 1872, President Ulysses Grant signed into law an act creating Yellowstone National Park.

In 1872 the vast wilderness of the west was viewed by most Americans as something to be tamed, to be explored, settled, mined, logged, ranched and farmed. For most at that time the west was not valued for its wilderness, but rather for the material treasures that it could yield. It is remarkable that during such an age Yellowstone was set aside as the world's first national park. That such a park could have been created more than a century ago is perhaps the most illustrative indicator of how unique and magnificent the Yellowstone country was perceived to be, even then.

Of the undisturbed, ecologically cohesive areas so common in western America in 1872, few remain. Now, at a time when the face of the earth has become so ravaged that few truly natural areas remain, the Yellowstone country assumes a value far greater than the original proponents of the national park ever could have anticipated. Here we find the largest essentially intact ecosystem remaining in the lower 48 states—millions of acres of diverse mountain wilderness relatively untouched by the imprint of man, much the same as it was hundreds, or even thousands, of years ago. Here in Yellowstone National Park and in the surrounding millions of acres of national forest, nearly every species of plant and animal life that John Colter could have seen when he ventured into the area almost 200 years ago continue to flourish.

But Yellowstone National Park is not an island. Geographically, biologically and ecologically it is part of and highly dependent upon millions of acres of adjacent lands, which together with the park itself comprise the "Greater Yellowstone" area. The environmental integrity of Yellowstone Park is dependent upon the careful management of these lands. In most instances the lands around Yellowstone must remain in a relatively natural condition for the biological community of Yellowstone itself to remain viable. Plants and animals do not recognize the politically-established park boundary. Some of man's activities on surrounding national forest, state and private lands, though politically apart from Yellowstone, pose severe threats to the wildlife, water, air, thermal features and other aspects of the park itself.

SHARON CUMMINGS/DEMBINSKY PHOTO ASSOC.

Twin Lakes, Yellowstone National Park. **Facing page:** *Camas lilies.*

YELLOWSTONE NATIONAL PARK

How did it happen that the Yellowstone country was singled out so many years ago for special status as the world's first national park? What made this area of the west so worthy of consideration in the 19th century and so famous in the 20th century?

From the very earliest visitation by white men it was evident that even by comparison to the enormous primeval American wilderness of the early 19th century, Yellowstone was special and in some ways unique. The wonders awaiting the early trappers, prospectors and other explorers who first saw Yellowstone were so incredible, so beyond belief, that when they returned to civilization to report their findings they frequently were regarded as outrageous liars. Their reports of fire, steam, seething earth, enormous waterfalls and petrified forests were so outlandish that the area was for decades discounted as a mythical place. But these men had seen what they said they had: explosive geysers, mud pots, boiling

DIANE STRATTON

pools, steam vents, cauldrons, sulphur pools, travertine springs and a variety of other phenomena. Had they covered the Yellowstone country entirely, they eventually would have encountered more than 300 geysers and nearly 10,000 other thermal features.

And there was more to the incredible geology of Yellowstone. Although no one could have known it at the time, modern geologists now know that the land across which the early trappers walked has been the site of some of the most massive explosive forces in the discernible geologic history of the planet. One such volcanic eruption left a caldera, a gigantic collapsed crater, some 45 miles wide. Neither could those explorers have known of the glaciers, earthquakes or lava flows that shaped Yellowstone, but we know of them today, and those who take time to learn of them will marvel.

Many contemporary visitors to Yellowstone confine themselves to roads and automobiles and pass through so quickly they fail to appreciate the real

Wednesday, August 31, 1870...Standing there or rather lying there for greater safety, I thought how utterly impossible it would be to describe to another the sensations inspired by such a presence. As I took in this scene, I realized my own littleness, my helplessness, my dread exposure to destruction, my inability to cope with or even comprehend the mighty architecture of nature. More than all this I felt as never before my entire dependence upon that Almighty Power who had wrought these wonders.

NATHANIEL P. LANGFORD

Below: *Boiling mudpots.*

Facing page: *The Firehole River as it meanders through Midway Geyser Basin.*

MICHAEL H. FRANCIS

significance of what they are seeing. Were they to spend the time, they would realize that Yellowstone is as unique biologically as it is geologically. The park, in combination with millions of acres of adjoining national forest, comprises what is perhaps the largest and most nearly intact ecosystem remaining in the contiguous United States. Across this region nature still reigns. The heavy imprint of human interference with naturally functioning biosystems has not yet been felt here.

Yellowstone, the world's first national park, has been designated by the United Nations as a World Heritage Site and an international Biosphere Reserve, recognized for the global value of its thermal features and natural ecosystem.

AND JUST BENEATH THE SURFACE AN UNEXPLODED NATURAL BOMB

At most places under the earth's crust molten material known as magma is 22 to 25 miles down; in some places beneath the deceptive coolness of Yellowstone it may be as near as fewer than two miles. Yellowstone may well be the hottest spot on earth. During the last 2 million years this hot fluid rock filled large chambers beneath the Yellowstone plateau. Now partially crystallized and solidified, it is still there and is still very hot. About 600,000 years ago this giant reservoir of molten rock pushed up near the surface, slowly bulging and then cracking the ground. Suddenly an extremely violent explosive eruption occurred in which hundreds of cubic miles of material were blown out. The force of that explosion can only be estimated from geologic evidence we discern today, but it was of such a magnitude that nothing during recorded human history approaches it. It was at least a thousand times more powerful than the explosion that blew the top off Washington's

Mount St. Helens in 1980. Airborne material from the blast came down at sites more than a thousand miles away; the enormous ash cloud must have dimmed the sun for months, on a global scale.

In the wake of this cataclysmic eruption the roofs of the twin magma chambers, which had vented to the surface, collapsed. The result was an immense caldera that sank several thousand feet into the earth across an area roughly 30 by 45 miles. Subsequently, more magma flowed upward and poured out, this time more quietly, eventually filling the floor of the smoldering caldera.

That was not the first time Yellowstone had exploded and it probably won't be the last. In recent geologic history we have evidence of similar activity 1.2 and 2 million years ago in and around Yellowstone. Today resurgent domes, bulges in the earth's surface, are rising in Yellowstone at an extremely rapid rate, geologically speaking. This high rate of uplift is comparable to that of the active volcanoes of Iceland and Hawaii.

What scientists call convective heat flow, or the amount of heat flowing out of an area, is extremely high throughout Yellowstone—more than 20 times higher than average heat flows elsewhere on the continent. In the upper geyser basin alone the amount of heat given off is 800 times greater than the amount given off by a nonthermal area of comparable size. It is this enormous heat source at very shallow depths beneath Yellowstone Park that accounts for the unique thermal features of the area.

Geothermal activity requires water, a heat source, and some mechanism for transferring heat to the water and allowing it to return to the surface. In Yellowstone all three conditions are met and together provide the world's greatest

PAT O'HARA

display of geothermal phenomena. Surface water from rain or snow is carried downward through cracks and faults in the earth where it comes in contact with magma-heated rocks. Most of the major thermal areas of Yellowstone are in proximity to the ring of fracture zones that formed around the rim of the Yellowstone caldera where deep cracks and faults act as passageways for surface water to reach the heat source. In other areas of the park, regional fault systems provide conduits for water. The water, sometimes heated to several hundred degrees Fahrenheit, then rises back to the surface, manifesting itself in a number of different ways depending on temperature, pressure, water chemistry and the nature of the fractures and conduits through which it flows. In Yellowstone the water emerges in powerful geysers, hot springs, steam fumaroles and mud pots, and in beautiful terraces from mineral-laden springs.

The thermal features of Yellowstone are unique—there is no parallel to their number and variety anywhere on earth. They are irreplaceable natural features. From experience in other areas of the world we know that such thermal features, especially geysers, are easily disturbed by geothermal exploration and production. Today Yellowstone is probably the only major undisturbed geyser field remaining on earth.

The volcanism that has so violently altered the face of Yellowstone in recent geologic times represents only the latest episode of a very long volcanic history in the area. Some 50 million years ago a number of large volcanoes erupted in the vicinity of Yellowstone Park. Many of these volcanoes were not the violent exploding type, but rather poured out vast quantities of lava and other material in giant flows that covered several thousand square miles to depths of many thousands of feet. This material comprises much of the Absaroka Range, which forms the northern and eastern portions of present-day Yellowstone National Park.

Intermittently these volcanoes coughed out vast clouds of hot ash, dust, steam, red-hot lava and rock fragments that buried everything in their path. It must have been much like the burial of the landscape around Mount St. Helens in 1980, but on a much larger scale. The sudden onset of so much volcanic material under just the right set of conditions buried trees and other plants under a blanket of ash and debris. Mineral-bearing waters flowing through the debris transformed buried plant material into fossils and petrified wood. For this to occur, burial had to be rapid enough to prevent decay and gentle enough not to destroy the fragile trees and plants. Water in the right

Below: The terraces of Mammoth Hot Springs, Yellowstone National Park.

Facing page: Yellowstone Lake's frozen winter patterns.

PAUL DIX

STEVEN FULLER

TOM MURPHY PHOTOS BOTH PAGES

West Boulder Falls in the Absaroka-Beartooth Wilderness Area.

A pack string passes Wall Mountain on Wyoming's Shoshone National Forest.

LIFE IN THE HOT POOLS

In a place such as Yellowstone where people have left nature largely unmolested, we stand to learn some of our greatest lessons. A case in point is the scientific findings that are emerging from our investigations of the life forms inhabiting the park's thermal environments

The vivid colors found in many of Yellowstone's thermal waters are caused by living organisms called "thermophilic life." Many of these organisms, both

plant and animal, are so perfectly adapted to their special thermal environments that they are found no place else.

Some bacteria can actually live in the boiling water of Yellowstone's thermal features. At temperatures below boiling, vast numbers of other micro-organisms flourish. The greatest number of microbes, both bacteria and algae, live in water between 122 and 140 degrees Fahrenheit. In the more moderate temperatures of hot-spring channels, some animal life is found. Ephydrid flies, for example, can survive continuously up to 109 degrees Fahrenheit feeding on the algae and bacteria of the thermal waters. Another fly, the dolichopodid, is a carnivorous

predator that eats the eggs and larvae of ephydrid flies. Life in the form of algae, bacteria and some ephydrid flies even survives in acid springs.

The life forms in such unusual environments may hold valuable secrets for man. These natural organisms may unlock new knowledge about life and its origin or may lead us to profoundly beneficial biological applications as in the case of the Sulfolobus acidocaldarius, a bacteria that obtains its energy by oxidizing sulfur. This organism, which thrives in a hot, acid environment and consumes sulfur, now helps man burn coal more cleanly. We can only speculate about the other secrets held by the life forms of Yellowstone's hot pools.

Queen's Lavatory hot pool. PETE & ALICE BENGEYFIELD

quantities and of the proper chemical composition and temperature also was required. In Yellowstone the conditions were just right to produce one of the most extensive petrified forests on earth.

The petrified forests of Yellowstone include many trees in upright positions, a rarity on such a vast scale. One geological interpretation of these forests is that they occur in layers, perhaps 27 in all, possibly indicating repeated cycles of forest growth, volcanic burial, more forest growth, more burial, and so on. Most unusual indeed! And because of the protection afforded by the creation of Yellowstone National Park 119 years ago, its petrified forests have been spared most of the vandalism and senseless destruction that have befallen similar features elsewhere in the world. Today these remarkable stone trees are there for all to see, reminders of the dramatic change that has come to the face of this landscape through the eons of time.

LETTING NATURE TAKE ITS COURSE: MANAGING YELLOWSTONE AS A NATURAL AREA

Although it was primarily the geologic and thermal features of Yellowstone that caught the people's interest and were largely responsible for the creation of the national park, in more recent times the fabulously abundant and diverse wildlife of the area also has captured the visitor's attention. On a knoll in the Lamar Valley of northeastern Yellowstone, for example, a small group of Yellowstone Institute participants gathered one June evening in 1981 to observe wildlife. In little more than an hour the group spotted elk, moose, mule deer, pronghorn antelope, bison, bighorn sheep, black bears and grizzlies. It may be

the only place on the face of the planet where this could be done, for where else does such a variety of animals share a common home except in this one valley of Yellowstone?

In the act of Congress that created Yellowstone National Park on March 1, 1872, it was specified that the area be dedicated and set apart "for the preservation, from injury or despoliation, of all timber, mineral deposits, natural curiosities, or wonders…and their retention in their natural condition." In modern times the National Park Service has taken seriously its mission of managing Yellowstone as a natural area. It has not always been this way, and some bad mistakes have been made in the past. Today enlightened park managers prefer a continually evolving policy of non-interference with the park's life forms and their natural environment. In practice this means allowing the predator-

In the adjacent mountains, beneath the living trees the edges of petrified forests are exposed to view, like specimens on the shelves of a museum, standing on ledges tier above tier where they grew, solemnly silent in rigid crystalline beauty after swaying in the winds thousands of centuries ago, opening marvelous views back into the years and climates and life of the past.

JOHN MUIR, 1898

Petrified trees on Specimen Ridge.   GEORGE WUERTHNER

Certainly it is the largest relatively intact ecosystem remaining in the lower 48 states, but it is tiny when compared to the rest of the nation. You can drive through the area in almost any direction in a few hours. It is the largest, but it is not large.

FRANZ CAMENZIND,
WYOMING BIOLOGIST

Below: *Catch-and-release fishing for rainbow trout.*

Facing page: *An osprey's catch-and-keep trout fishing on the Snake River.*

DENNIS HENRY

prey relationship to operate free of interference; allowing the natural forces of winter kill and the carrying capacity of the range to control wildlife numbers; allowing naturally caused fires to burn; avoiding the use of herbicides or pesticides to manipulate the environment and routing humans away from sensitive wildlife areas.

But allowing nature to take its course in Yellowstone is not quite as simple as it may sound, for even though the overwhelming majority of Yellowstone is still wild, the park is not pristine. During the 1980s, an average of 2.17 million people pass through Yellowstone each year and within the park itself there are several major developments including hotels, cabins, restaurants, marinas, campgrounds, curio shops and service stations to accommodate and feed thou-

sands of park visitors and employees every day. Amazingly, park developments including roads, power lines and sewage systems occupy less than one percent of the total park acreage, but human presence is felt far beyond those areas.

Yellowstone is not entirely pristine in other ways. The natural role of fire was suppressed for many decades in Yellowstone, giving rise to altered forest and plant communities in some areas of the park. Exotic plant species such as timothy and Canadian thistle are widespread and many other exotics occur locally in a variety of locations, especially along the roadside and in areas such as the Lamar Valley, which was under cultivation during the days of the bison ranching there.

The policy of non-interference should not be confused with the policy of no management. Regulations that keep people from disturbing nesting pelicans are "management"; so is the vigorous denial of human garbage to bears, or the closing of grizzly-inhabited trails to hikers.

A large number of cutthroat trout in Yellowstone Lake are naturally infested with fish tapeworms and were so long before the arrival of white man. The tapeworms are ugly little devils that crawl out of the fish flesh and across the frying pan when fishers are cooking up the morning catch. At another time and in a different place, man might have attempted to eradicate the tapeworm as a "bad" organism parasitic on "good" fish. Under the non-interference policy of Yellowstone, however, the tapeworm is allowed to fulfill its biological role.

We've had a chance in Yellowstone to observe the life cycle of a tapeworm and have discovered some fascinating connections. The adult lives in the digestive tract of Yellowstone Lake birds such as pelicans, gulls, ospreys and others.

JEFF VANUGA

The eggs of the tapeworm are carried in the droppings of these birds, most of which end up in the lake where they are eaten by small fresh-water shrimp; the shrimp in turn are eaten by fish where the tapeworm lodges itself in the flesh. To complete the cycle, the birds, at the top of the food chain, eat the fish. What role the tapeworm plays in its hosts is not known, but it is a natural phenomenon that here is allowed to function without interference by man. And so it is with nearly everything in Yellowstone.

In the past non-interference with nature has not always been practiced in Yellowstone. This frequently has yielded colossal blunders, such as the war on predators described in the story on wolves (see page 76). At other times interference with nature has had results that, today at least, seem desirable. One such episode lasting more than half a century occurred with the feeding and full-scale ranching of bison. But that interference with nature was undertaken in the name of restoring a creature nearly eliminated by an earlier human misdeed.

Another example of management interfer-

HENRY H. HOLDSWORTH

MICHAEL H. FRANCIS

ence to correct the results of earlier actions can be seen in the highly controversial Yellowstone bear policy. For 80 years bears in Yellowstone feasted on garbage, which had become the major food source for many park bears. Several large open-dump sites in and immediately adjacent to the park became congregating locations, especially for grizzlies. On one night in 1966, for example, 88 grizzlies were observed at the Trout Creek dump. Park bears also obtained human food from other sources: anywhere there were garbage cans, in campers' coolers, and along the roadsides, where eager visitors fed begging black bears.

In 1967, the National Park Service began to deny garbage and other human food to bears. By the fall of 1970 the park's open-pit garbage dumps were closed; by 1971 garbage cans were bear-proofed and rules regulating food storage in campgrounds were implemented. This was a manage-

ment decision to interfere with long established, but nevertheless unnatural, feeding habits of the bear. The policy caused a storm of controversy and was opposed vigorously by bear researchers John and Frank Craighead, who argued that sudden denial of garbage would have disastrous consequences on the Yellowstone grizzly population. Now more than 15 years later, the jury is still out on the dump controversy, but recent data is very encouraging. In 1990, 24 unduplicated female grizzlies with cubs were seen in the Greater Yellowstone Ecosystem. There were 57 cubs with these females, the largest number of cubs known to be reproduced in the ecosystem in any one year. Average litter size is also on the rise and in 1990 stood at the highest average since 1968.

In the recent past, some persons have proposed that supplemental feeding of grizzly bears in Yellowstone is necessary during periods of critical

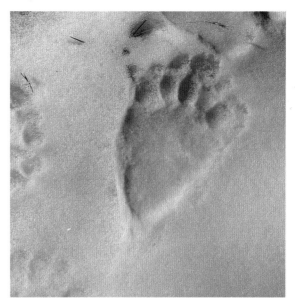

STEVEN FULLER

HENRY H. HOLDSWORTH

Left: *To humans of all time, the grizzly has been the Great Bear.*
Above: *Grizzly prints.*

Facing page: *A radio-collared grizzly sow with cubs, and park service staff transporting a drugged grizzly.*

natural food shortages. Many bear biologists oppose supplemental feeding and share the concern expressed by Chris Servheen, grizzly-bear specialist for the U.S. Fish and Wildlife Service, when he asks, "Do we want grizzly bears if the only way to have them is to feed them in a big pile?" But right or wrong, a deliberate manipulation of the natural ecosystem was proposed as one way to restore a healthy bear population. So while the official management policy for Yellowstone National Park today is to let nature take its course without human interference, in some cases (such as the elimination of wolves, the denial of historic winter range, or the garbage-hooked bears) people have so altered natural systems that we must re-interfere to try to restore them. It remains to be seen if this can ever be fully achieved, but if it can, it's likely that Yellowstone is where it will happen.

Greater Yellowstone is large enough, remote enough, diverse enough, and, with the exception of wildlife poaching, protected enough to provide most, and in some cases all, of the necessary ingredients for a smoothly functioning, self-regulating ecosystem. Presumably if people pulled out of the area today, totally absenting themselves from 5 or 6 million acres, native plant and animal life forms would continue to survive, even flourish. That is so because sufficient area remains in a natural condition for self-sustaining, self-balancing natural forces to function. This isn't true of most areas in America today—humans have so interfered with their environment that they are now compelled to hold it together by ever more artificial means: by building dams to control floods caused by our destruction of watershed; by using

Sandhill cranes.

TOM MURPHY

An Indian paintbrush surrounded by bluebells—typical of the Greater Yellowstone Ecosystem.

PAT O'HARA

pesticides to control insects which are out of control because we have destroyed the creatures that prey on them; by poisoning coyotes because they are eating sheep because we have poisoned the rodents which were the coyote's primary food source, and so on.

That natural systems continue to function fairly well in Greater Yellowstone in the 1990s is no accident. Historically Yellowstone Park itself has been protected by its national park status against a host of threats. Much of the rest of Greater Yellowstone has been afforded some political protection in forest reserves, national wildlife refuges and in Grand Teton National Park. Topography, climate and remoteness also have played some role in protecting the area.

In the last several decades, however, much of Greater Yellowstone has come under commodity-producing pressures, notably from large-scale timber and mineral development and sharply increasing numbers of people. Until very recently, the plant and animal life of the park was still relatively secure because habitats were secure, but as pressures on surrounding lands intensify the effect is being felt deep inside Yellowstone.

Portions of Yellowstone Park are covered with vegetation to support up to 25,000 elk on various summer ranges. But this is high country, and heavy snows blanket it for more than half the year. Thus, the real carrying capacity of the land is determined by its scarce winter range. Some of it lies beyond the park boundary on surrounding national forest and private lands. This winter range is essential to the Yellowstone elk herds, but it is beyond the geographical and in most cases the political control of National Park Service managers. Fortunately, private organizations such as the Rocky Mountain Elk Foundation and progressive public agencies such as the Montana Department of Fish, Wildlife and Parks and the Forest Service are purchasing some of this property for elk winter range, but much more needs to be done. The same thing can be said to a lesser extent for others of Yellowstone's wildlife species. Grizzly bears range widely beyond the park, mule deer and bighorn sheep cross freely back and forth across park boundaries, bald eagles, trumpeter swans and pelicans cover hundreds, sometimes thousands, of miles outside the park each year. Yellowstone Park itself simply is not large enough to provide all that its creatures require.

Commercial logging and, with a few small exceptions, domestic livestock grazing have never been permitted in Yellowstone Park. As a result plant communities here present us with a relatively good picture of the natural processes of plant succession. As in the case of Yellowstone's wildlife, human interference with plant life has been felt to a degree through such practices as fire suppression, some limited farming, a pesticide attack on insects and a few other intrusions, but plant life in most of Yellowstone today is probably as natural as any to be found. There are about 1,000 species of flowering plants and 13 species of trees in the park, not a particularly diverse plant community, but not surprising in light of the history of recent volcanism and glaciation and the

high elevations. Eighty percent of Yellowstone is forested. Of the tree species found in the park eight are coniferous, and of those the lodgepole pine is by far the most common.

The special relationship between fire and the lodgepole pine is yet another of the remarkable natural dramas that we can observe in Yellowstone. (See section on fire, page 43.) The lodgepole thrives in post-fire environments and many have what are called serotinous cones, which release seeds in the heat of a fire to regenerate new forests. Other species occur only in post-fire environments where increased sunlight and reduced competition for nutrients contribute to the growth of shrubs, wildflowers, berries and vigorous stands of new trees. Many animals and birds also do well in burned-over areas, as new sources of forage and nesting sites for birds are provided.

For many years, man attempted to suppress

TOM MURPHY

W. PERRY CONWAY

After the fires of 1988:
Right: *A lodgepole seedling rises among charred trunks.*

Above: *In June 1989, this lodgepole forest showed the various degrees of fire's effect.*

natural lightning-caused fires in western forests, and Yellowstone was no exception. With the advent of fire patrols by aircraft in the 1950s, fire suppression became far more effective. For a period of about 20 years fire was not allowed to play its role as a thinning agent in Yellowstone. It is estimated that about 10 percent of all the park's lodgepole was affected. During the past decade the National Park Service has adopted a natural-burn policy for lightning-caused fires that do not threaten man or property in the park. Many fires have been allowed to run their course under this policy and in most instances fire is once again playing its role in Yellowstone's forests.

There is something in Yellowstone's forests now allowed to run its natural course: insect infestations. In recent years tens of thousands of Yellowstone lodgepoles have been killed by an infestation of mountain pine beetles, which bore into trees and so diminish their flow of resin that they die. For several years park managers fought the beetle infestation in an effort to "save" the forests. The battle was eventually abandoned, perhaps as much for its futility as for the emerging recognition that the beetle epidemics were a natural phenomenon that played a positive role in the complex scheme of energy exchanges occurring in the forest. The beetles here are as natural and as much a part of the forest as the lodgepole. We can't exterminate the beetles and call Yellowstone "natural" any more than we can exterminate the lodgepole and call it "natural." To the casual observer, a forest under attack by the beetle may appear to be annihilated, but this is not so. In fact, the beetle infestation is highly selective, affecting primarily older, mature trees and ignoring the younger ones. The inner bark of young, healthy trees is too thin for beetles to survive.

The beetles come and go in cycles that are

CARL R. SAMS II/DEMBINSKY PHOTO ASSOC.

dependent upon favorable weather conditions and food supply. They are, along with fire, nature's way of thinning the forest and allowing younger trees to flourish. Beetle-killed trees are not wasted. Their snags provide perching and nesting sites for hawks and eagles and for cavity-nesting birds such as the mountain bluebird. The forest floor is transformed, ground nesting birds find protected nest sites and other forms of wildlife find greater cover and feeding opportunities. Many of the birds that benefit from the altered forest prey on beetles; browse, berries and forage appear where none was found before. The self-regulating capacity of nature's way has worked its magic.

In myriad ways, similar mechanisms are at work in Yellowstone's spruce-fir forest, alpine tundra, marshland, sagebrush-grassland and aquatic plant communities. In Yellowstone where the heavy imprint of man's interference has not yet been felt, we can still see the functioning of these natural marvels and develop an appreciation for the interrelatedness of the natural world and of our very modest place in it as just one among God's creatures.

Bull elk.

YELLOWSTONE PARK, THE WORLD HERITAGE SITE

What does Yellowstone have in common with Australia's Great Barrier Reef, Equador's Galapagos Islands, Egypt's pyramids, Nepal's Katmandu Valley, Tanzania's Serengeti, the historic center of Rome, and the Palace of Versailles? The answer: All are areas of such extraordinary natural or cultural significance that they, along with more than a hundred other places, have been designated World Heritage Sites by the UNESCO World Heritage Committee of the United Nations.

Some 53 nations participate in this program, which is intended to identify and protect those natural and cultural areas of the earth that are of outstanding universal value to all the peoples of the world—areas whose loss or diminution would be felt by all who share a common human history and a limited living space on our fragile planet.

In 1978, the U.N. World Heritage Committee initiated Yellowstone National Park into membership in the exclusive club of world heritage sites. Yellowstone was the first American natural area selected.

Yellowstone hot springs.

ALAN & SANDY CAREY

TOM MURPHY

YELLOWSTONE PARK, THE WORLD BIOSPHERE RESERVE

In 1971, the United Nations Educational, Social and Cultural Organization (UNESCO) acting in a time of what it perceived to be urgent need, embarked upon a program to identify, recognize and promote the conservation of outstanding representative examples of the world's major ecosystems and their components. The project, under the auspices of UNESCO's Man and the Biosphere Program, was an attempt to conserve the dwindling genetic material of the earth's life forms in order to provide a future of maximum global genetic diversity.

It is indicative of its great geological and biological significance that in 1972, Yellowstone was the first area in America to be designated a biosphere reserve. There are now 209 biosphere reserves in 55 countries around the world. "Conserving the Unknown" UNESCO calls it—unknown because when such areas are destroyed we don't know what we're losing in species and in the information they hold; unknown because we don't know what our future perceptions will be of what is a pleasant and livable world.

Those are questions of global concern that go far beyond America's borders.

Bison bull.

MICHAEL H. FRANCIS

Glacial boulders in the Lamar Valley under the smoke of 1988. **Facing page:** *Frost on a burned lodgepole pine.*

FIRES IN THE GREATER YELLOWSTONE ECOSYSTEM

by George Wuerthner

During the summer of 1988, wildfires burned through approximately 1.4 million acres in the Greater Yellowstone Ecosystem (map, page 49), capturing national attention and unleashing a firestorm of debate about firepolicy as well as the role of natural wildfire in the ecosystem. Many people criticized Yellowstone National Park managers, suggesting that they acted irresponsibly by allowing fires to burn. What was not widely reported in the media was that nearly all wildfires were fought from the moment they were discovered, especially once it appeared that 1988's conditions would be different from those of previous years. Despite this herculean fire suppression effort, wildfires burned out of control for weeks on end. One of the lessons learned was that human efforts to control nature sometimes

PERRY CONWAY

still fail in extraordinary circumstances. The summer of 1988 was extraordinary for many reasons.

In most years, the forests of the Greater Yellowstone Ecosystem are virtually flameproof. The generally high elevations of the ecosystem retains snow cover for eight to nine months of the year, and by the time the forests dry out enough to burn, usually about mid- to late August, new storms begin to pile up the next season's snow. Computer modeling of climatic conditions and other factors have demonstrated that in most years Yellowstone simply could not burn—even if you wanted to set the place on fire.

This is borne out by fire history records. Scientists can determine such history by studying fire scars on old trees. By counting tree rings and the occurrence of scar tissue on many trees, it is possible to construct

Nature has all the regenerative potential it needs for these ecosystems, without human interference.

NORMAN L. CHRISTENSEN,
DUKE UNIVERSITY
BOTANIST AND
CHAIRMAN OF THE PARK'S
POST-FIRE ECOLOGICAL
ASSESSMENT COMMITTEE

Right: *Road closed, 1988.*

Facing page: *Lightning storm east of Livingston shows the main cause of fire in the Greater Yellowstone Ecosystem.*

the fire history of a particular region. These studies have shown that large fires, in fact some much larger than those in 1988, are a regular feature of the Greater Yellowstone Ecosystem, occurring at infrequent intervals of 200 to 400 years. The exceptions to this general rule are the drier, lower-elevation grasslands and forest savanna areas where fires burned at a frequency of only 20-year intervals.

Bear in mind that these are averages. An area might not burn for 50 years, then, because of severe drought conditions, it could burn three times in 10 years. This would give a 20-year fire interval, but timing of fires of course occurs in more irregular fashion than the average suggests.

Fire history research here also demonstrated that the last big fires in the ecosystem occurred in the 1750s and 1850s. After 200 years without a major fire, fuels had accumulated, making large blazes possible. There has been sufficient fuel in much of Yellowstone since the 1930s to carry a big fire. (Note: In other ecosystems with different climatic conditions and fire history, 40 or 50 years of fire suppression could be significant.)

But fuels are not the only reason for major blazes. Another factor that increases the likelihood of a conflagration is the understory invasion of predominantly lodgepole pine forests by the slow-growing and shade-tolerate subalpine fir. Subalpine fir is highly flammable, and its growth habitat is such that it has branches from the ground to its crown. This provides a natural ladder for flames to climb into the top of the forest canopy, where they can jump easily from tree to tree, or "crown out," as firefighters say. A subalpine fir understory normally takes 150 to 300 years to develop—and without it, fires have a more difficult time spreading over wide areas.

In most years, lightning—the usual ignition source—starts dozens of fires in the Greater Yel-

lowstone Ecosystem. Nearly all of these go out on their own after burning only a few acres at most—even without suppression efforts—simply because conditions for a major blaze do not exist. For instance, in Yellowstone Park between 1972 and 1987 there were 233 lightning-caused blazes that burned without any attempt at suppression. Of these, 205 fizzled out without burning an acre. Of the remainder, only a few actually burned more than a few hundred acres.

Fire research, not only in Yellowstone, but throughout the West, has documented similar trends and promulgated several general principles. First, the vast majority of fires go out on their own, whether people do anything or not. At least in the Greater Yellowstone Ecosystem, one can generalize by saying that under normal environmental cir-

BARBARA & MICHAEL PFLAUM

TOM MURPHY

Yellowstone was a ticking time bomb....We had old brush, old timber: 150- to 200-year-old trees. And that's historic when they start burning.

FIREFIGHTER PATRICK PONTES, QUOTED IN ROSS SIMPSON'S *THE FIRES OF '88*

cumstances fire suppression efforts are wasted. The second principle is that the vast majority of acreage charred in any fire season occurs in a handful of large fires that, for one reason or another, are able to persist and grow. And finally, the specter raised by the fires of 1988 is that, when conditions are adverse to fire suppression efforts, no amount of human intervention can stop the blazes.

All these basic principles were seen during the 1988 fire season. During that summer, there were 249 fires in the Greater Yellowstone area, yet 201 burned only 10 acres or fewer. But the few that grew beyond this size quickly became monsters. The largest was the massive 504,025-acre North Fork fire. Other large burns included the 319,575-acre Clover-Mist fire and the 227,525-acre Huck fire. Of the total 1.4 million-acre fire perimeter, some 989,000 acres were within Yellowstone National Park.

It is important to note that most of these fires burned in a mosaic pattern, and that much of the area remained unburned within any single fire perimeter. The acreage figures represent the total *outer extent* of fire advance, not the total acres actually burned. Furthermore, many acres were only lightly charred, converting litter and duff to ashes, but not necessarily killing all trees or other plants. Only 22,000 acres, or less than one percent of the park, experienced what ecologists call a "hot" fire, destroying soil horizons and volatilizing nutrients.

At one point, nearly 10,000 people joined in the fire-fighting force that included both civilian and military units, dozens of helicopters and more than a hundred fire trucks. Some 665 miles of fire line were dug by hand, and another 137 miles constructed by bulldozer. But many fire fighters later joked that the only fire line that the flames did not jump was 14-mile-wide Yellowstone Lake.

Right top: *A firefighter on the Storm Creek fire needs to filter the sooty air for breathing.*
Center: *Night-time made the flames look especially spectacular.*
Bottom: *A burned sign proclaims that once a trail passed this way.*

Facing page: *Helicopters ferried gigantic buckets of Yellowstone Lake water constantly.*

MICHAEL CRUMMETT

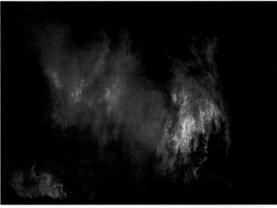
BARBARA & MICHAEL PFLAUM

W. PERRY CONWAY

Fires threatened communities like West Yellowstone and Cooke City and nearly overran developments at Old Faithful. A couple dozen cabins were burned, primarily on the eastern edge of the fires along the Shoshone National Forest boundary, but the loss of lives and property, given the magnitude of the blazes, was incredibly small. But there were some costs to bear, including the unfortunate accidental deaths of two fire fighters and the $120 million price tag for suppression efforts.

Yet, for all the money spent and effort exerted, those fighting the flames, as well as informed ecologists and fire managers, generally believed that these massive efforts did not significantly lessen the acreage burned. Five out of the eight major fires in the ecosystem were fought hard from the minute they were discovered—but with no real effect. Snow on September 10, not fire fighters, brought the historic blazes under control.

Though these were extraordinary fires of a historic scale, from an ecological perspective they did no damage to the Greater Yellowstone Ecosystem. Some would argue that Yellowstone's forests are not "recovering," but merely going through one part of a long and repeated cycle of burn followed by regrowth, only to burn once more. In many instances, according to the Greater Yellowstone Coordinating Committee, a group of National Forest, National Park and other federal land managing agencies guiding management in the Greater Yellowstone area, "the efforts of fighting the fires created more enduring disruptions of settings than did the fires."

For example, three years after the fires, I saw bulldozed fire lines on the Blacktail Plateau marked by a swath of weeds, while adjacent burned areas had grown back to native grass and forbs. The long-term biological consequences of weed invasion is a much more serious threat to Yellowstone's ecolog-

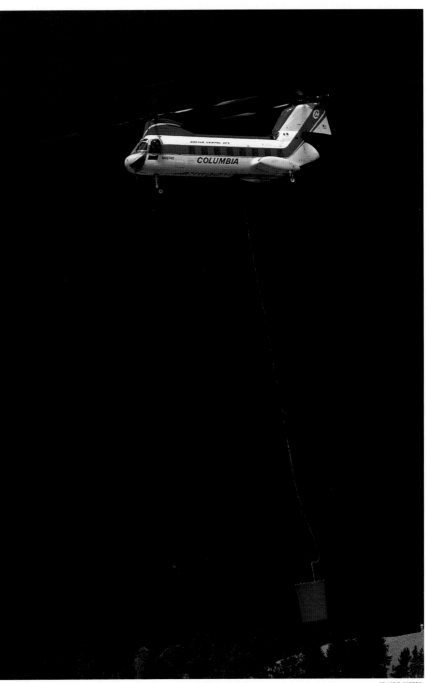

CRAIG R. HOBBS

ical integrity than the impacts of the fires themselves.

UNIQUE FACTORS IN 1988

Several factors led up to this historic fire event. Severe and prolonged drought is one. The summer of 1988 was the driest on record in the park's 112-year existence. Not only was the summer of 1988 dry, but it culminated a record-breaking drought that began in the fall of 1986. Below-average snow pack in the mountains followed by hot, dry summers led up to the summer of '88. But even under these severe conditions, at least 11 of 20 lightning-caused blazes went out themselves.

However, no rain fell in June, July and August—an almost unheard-of situation—and by late July, moisture content of grasses and tinder was as low as 2 to 3 percent (kiln-dried lumber is 12 percent). Night-time humidity during much of the fire season was also very low, allowing fires to burn throughout the nights, when most flames die down under normal circumstances.

But drought is not the only requirement for a large blaze. As we have seen, the necessary abundance of fuels awaited in the Greater Yellowstone Ecosystem.

Topographic features also helped increase the spread of the blazes. Much of Yellowstone Park is a high, flat, forested plateau—the bottom of an ancient volcanic caldera—with a nearly continuous forest cover. Once a blaze got roaring, there was little in the way of topographical breaks such as major treeless alpine areas or rugged rocky canyons to slow the advance of flames.

In addition to fuels and drought, fire needs a source of ignition. In spite of the drought, dry thunderstorms occurred with greater frequency in 1988 and lightning strikes were double their normal amount. Lightning was responsible for five out of the eight major fire complexes.

Several fires also were ignited by human carelessness. The massive North Fork fire, largest in the ecosystem, was started by a woodcutter outside the park, who discarded a cigarette. The Hellroaring Fire, another major blaze, started at an outfitter's camp in the Absaroka-Beartooth Wilderness north of the park. A third, the Huck Fire, began when a tree fell across a power line. During the course of the summer, nearly 40 percent of all fires, including three of the largest blazes, were started by human, not natural, causes. All were subject to immediate suppression efforts, but with little success.

Even under drought conditions, with plenty of fuel and ignitions, a major conflagration might not arise. The fourth required ingredient is wind. Winds fan the flames, and carry embers far beyond the fire's perimeter, causing spotting, which ignites new blazes ahead of the main fire line. Spotting in 1988 made fire lines—even those constructed by bulldozers—impossible to hold. Winds regularly carried burning coals and brands up to a mile or more beyond the fire front, allowing the fires to jump not only fire lines, but even major topographic features such as the mile-wide Grand Canyon of the Yellowstone.

Gale-force winds made fire advances of 10 or more miles a day common. One wind-generated run of the Storm Creek Fire raced nine miles in just four hours. On August 20, gale force winds of 60 miles per hour helped the fires char more than 150,000 acres in a single day! Nearly half the acreage burned was burned on only four days of particularly high winds.

Many fire ecologists feel that under such conditions of drought, abundant fuel, low humidi-

PETE & ALICE BENGEYFIELD

JEFF VANUGA

This is one of those once-in-50-years, once-in-100-years deals.

> SECRETARY
> OF AGRICULTURE
> RICHARD LYNG IN
> WEST YELLOWSTONE, 1988

Left: *A just-erupted wall of flame sends firefighters retreating toward Canyon Village.*

Facing page: *This young elk faced a hard winter after the fires.*

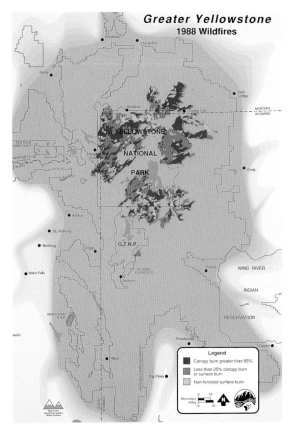

The falls, canyons, rivers and wildlife are still here, and by the time kids who come to the park in the near future return again, the trees will be taller than they will be.

STEVE TEDDER OF TW
SERVICES, FALL 1988

Views from the same spot in August 1988 (top), October 1988 (center) and August 1989 (bottom) show the extremely dry conditions of that summer, the very beginnings of regrowth, and what only a year meant around one stand of aspens.

CHARLES KAY PHOTOS

ty, numerous ignition sources combined with high winds, almost nothing can prevent a major forest fire. Certainly it was not fire fighting efforts that finally put out the flames, but the change in natural conditions on September 10, when snowfall and the cold nights of the autumn season finally brought the fires under control.

ECOLOGICAL CONSEQUENCES OF FIRES

Increasingly, scientists have recognized the important ecological role of fire in the West. Some ecologists even suggest that fires be permitted to burn (with proper protection for life and property) and that periodic large fires are not only desirable, but also necessary. In other words, the ecological effect of one large fire is significantly different than if the same acreage burned in numerous small blazes spread out over a century or more.

One of the major roles seen for fires is the recycling of nutrients that over time become locked up in dead litter and snags. In shallow soils, this nutrient bank—stored in dead material and unavailable for new plant growth—is frequently necessary for the future growth and health of the plant communities.

Unlike conditions in warm and humid climates (such as in the eastern United States) where dead trees, downed snags, fallen leaves and pine needles decompose rapidly as a result of bacteria and fungal activity, climatic conditions in the forest and meadows of the Greater Yellowstone hamper biological decomposition due to the long periods of winter cold and snow at high elevations, and by summer drought conditions that characterize low elevations. As a consequence, dead litter and snags rot very slowly. In the absence of rapid biological decomposition, it is fire that recharges the forest nutrient cycles.

Although very hot fires can volatilize (in effect, remove) important nutrients like nitrogen, the overall effect of most blazes is to release nutrients bound up in dead litter, making them available for new plant growth. New sources of nitrogen, for example, are quickly produced by nitrogen fixing bacteria and plants that recolonize recently charred soils.

When ash and other residues of the fires are carried into waterways, they also enrich nutrients in aquatic ecosystems. Some scientists speculate this enrichment may be critical to the long-term productivity of Yellowstone's outstanding fisheries.

Since not all trees usually are killed within a burn, fires are natural thinning agents. The remaining trees, released from competition, grow faster and are better able to withstand normal environmental stresses whether that be disease, drought or insects. Fire also prevents the invasion of meadows by forests. Grasses rapidly recover from fires and they tolerate periodic fires better than trees, helping to maintain grasslands, particularly at drier, lower elevations.

The snags created by fires also serve an important ecological purpose. Fully one quarter of the bird species in the region depend upon cavities for nesting, including bluebirds, woodpeckers, nuthatches and even some owl species. Since snags may remain upright for a century or more, wildfires ensure a steady supply of potential cavity sites for these species as well as other animals that utilize cavities, such as flying squirrels and bats.

The value of snags does not end when they fall down. Snags on the ground provide hiding cover for voles, mice and other small mammals. If the snags happen to topple into streams, they provide structural stability to streambanks as well as hiding cover for fish.

Few animals were killed by the 1988 Yellowstone fires, despite their size. Most small mammals could burrow into the ground, avoiding the heat of the blaze, while most large mammals and birds merely moved away from the flames. There is no way to determine how many smaller creatures like mice died in the blazes, but no more than 300 larger mammals perished in the flames. However, the loss of food coupled with already low forage production due to drought conditions combined to promote a major die-off of 8,000 to 10,000 elk the following winter. It is important to note that drought conditions were largely responsible for these deaths, because fires burned only a third of the winter range. Again, harsh as it may seem, this is a natural thinning process that keeps big-game herds in balance with available food supplies. But, the rejuvenation of rangelands and abundance of forage created by the fires likely will increase big game herds in the future.

FIRE-ADAPTED VEGETATION

Given that fires are a common and expected environmental feature in the Greater Yellowstone Ecosystem, it is not surprising that many plants are adapted to take advantage of these pyrotechnic events.

The most common conifer species in the region is lodgepole pine. Lodgepole has a number of adaptations that allow it to regenerate quickly after a blaze. The numerous occurrences of nearly even-aged stands established after previous fires throughout this ecosystem are testimony to lodgepole's persistence in the face of repeated fires.

Among its adaptations to fires are serotinous cones. Seeds are released from serotinous cones only after they have been singed or heated. Not all lodgepole cones are serotinous; in fact, most of the

Fires are as much a part of the ecosystem as snow, wind and rain.

PROF. WILLIAM H. ROMME
FORT LEWIS COLLEGE,
DURANGO, COLORADO

Below: *Spring and summer of 1989 brought colorful, stunning contrasts of new growth amidst ashes.*

Facing page: *Burn patterns on Mt. Bunsen.*

DIANA STRATTON

trees in Yellowstone have predominantly non-serotinous cones. However, the few cones that remain unopened until a fire ensure that there will always be an abundant seed source to restock a burned site.

Lodgepole pine also grows best in full open sunshine—the condition that prevails after a fire. They grow rapidly, and mature early. A five-year-old lodgepole pine sapling is capable of bearing cones with viable seeds, but other tree species may require a half century before they produce their first cones.

Self-pruning is another adaptation widely seen, particularly in crowded lodgepole stands. There will be few branches on the lower trunks of trees. With no branches to carry flames up into the canopy, a ground fire will merely smolder through a lodgepole stand killing only young saplings, but not mature trees.

Another fire-adapted species is aspen. Aspen is a deciduous tree that has clean white boles with leafy, open canopies. The leaves turn a brilliant gold in the autumn, adding much color to the Greater Yellowstone Ecosystem. Under normal conditions, few aspens germinate from seeds. Most aspen regeneration is from suckers—branches that grow from roots when the main stem has died or been cut off. As many as 60,000 aspen suckers have been counted per acre after a fire. Of course, most of them do not survive. Elk and domestic cattle that graze Forest Service lands outside the park browse on aspen suckers, and in many areas they have totally eliminated aspen reproduction. However, so many new aspen shoots may develop as a result of the massive fires that browsing by wildlife and stock may not remove all new growth.

Another surprising find by scientists after the 1988 fires was the establishment of many young aspens from seeds. For years, ecologists thought that nearly all aspen regeneration came from suckers, so the discovery of significant production from seeds shed new light into aspen ecology. Although no one knows exactly why so many aspen seeds successfully germinated and grew, some suspect the environmental conditions provided by the fire may explain the phenomenon: nutrient-rich soil and extensive reduction of litter allowing seeds' rootlets to penetrate the bare soil.

Aspen is not the only species that sprouts from roots. Willow, rabbitbrush, some species of sagebrush, and other plants are all root sprouters and have regenerated quickly after the 1988 fires. Grass roots are seldom killed by fires, so regrowth in meadows is rapid and lush. In addition, many flowers, fertilized by the ash and released from shading by conifer canopy, have carpeted many forest floors with a rich abundance of blooms.

By the third summer after the fire, many

meadow areas of the park were completely reveg-etated and it was sometimes difficult to tell that they had burned. In other areas, particularly at higher elevations, regrowth is slower due to the shorter season—and evidence of the fires, partic-ularly snags, may remain for a century or more.

THE NECESSITY OF WILDFIRE

Wildfires are a necessary component of the Greater Yellowstone Ecosystem. Just as the tropical rainforest is adapted to deluges of rain and cannot exist without it, the plant communities of the Greater Yellowstone area are dependent upon wildfires for their ecological health and well being. If one wishes to preserve the park, one must pre-serve the processes that influence and shape it. When visitors gaze out on the pleasing park scen-ery, they are enjoying a largely fire-created vista. The fires of 1988 were not a natural disaster, but a major creative force for the park's ecological future.

One of the greatest values of large, undevel-oped landscapes like the Greater Yellowstone Eco-system is that natural, self-regulating forces like wildfires can be permitted to play their roles with little interference from modern human technology. Given the relative handful of places where this is still possible, just the scientific knowledge we may gain about fire behavior and the ecological role of fires makes the Greater Yellowstone Ecosystem a national asset.

STAN OSOLINSKI

PETE & ALICE BENGEYFIELD

The Gibbon River. **Facing page:** *Indian paintbrush.*

BEYOND YELLOWSTONE PARK
GREATER YELLOWSTONE DEFINED

The vastness of Yellowstone National Park is deceiving, for although it covers some 3,500 square miles, it is not large enough to survive independently and apart from its biological, ecological and geological context. As we already have noted the park is not an island, and nature does not recognize the lines we have drawn on the map and call park boundaries.

In some very important respects, activities on the lands surrounding Yellowstone National Park pose severe threats to wildlife, thermal features, air, water and other aspects of Yellowstone itself. The environmental integrity of the park depends on careful management of these lands, most of which must remain in an essentially natural condition to protect Yellowstone.

The boundaries that Congress created for Yellowstone National Park were drawn to include the thermal features of the area and Yellowstone Lake, but largely ignored biological considerations. We have learned much since that time. When Congress enact-

PAT O'HARA

ed the Alaska National Interest Lands Conservation Act in 1980, emphasis was placed on trying to draw park and wildlife refuge boundaries to include entire ecosystems. Yellowstone's boundaries were drawn in 1872 as a simple giant rectangle approximately 62 by 54 miles, containing well over 2 million acres. The concepts of watershed, wildlife migration routes, biological communities and intact ecosystems were not known at that time. Geology more than biology was the main criterion for the establishment of the park boundary.

It didn't take long, however, for some observers to recognize that Yellowstone's boundaries did not make much sense on the ground. General Philip H. Sheridan, the Civil War hero who visited Yellowstone in 1882, suggested then that the size of the park be vastly increased to extend beyond the existing boundaries 40 miles to the east and 10 miles to the south in order to encompass a more cohesive wildlife reserve. Although Sheridan's suggestion was never acted upon, there was considerable discussion about expanding

DENNIS J. CWIDAK

Above: *Upper Mesa Falls, Idaho.*
Right: *Bison crossing the Gardner River in Yellowstone National Park.*

Facing page: *The Snake River and the Grand Tetons.*

W. PERRY CONWAY

the park boundary during the next 50 years. In 1917, Secretary of the Interior Franklin Lane recommended a large addition to Yellowstone that would have encompassed the Teton Mountain Range, Jackson Hole and much of what we know today as the Teton Wilderness. Lane's proposal would have added 1,200 square miles to Yellowstone National Park, and it came very close to receiving congressional approval.

In the meantime several presidents empowered by the Forest Reserve Act of 1891 had created large forest reserves on land east and south of Yellowstone. In 1891, President Benjamin Harrison signed an order creating a "public forest reservation" known as the Yellowstone National Park Timberland Reserve along all of the east and a portion of the south park boundary. Six years later President Grover Cleveland set aside the Teton Forest Reserve, encompassing much of the Jackson Hole country. In 1902 both areas were expanded significantly by President Theodore Roosevelt. Almost all of these lands have since become part of the national forest system or have been integrated into Grand Teton National Park.

Although General Sheridan early recognized that the boundaries of Yellowstone Park didn't correspond to the distribution of its wildlife populations, it probably didn't make much difference in 1882. The law creating Yellowstone did little to protect the wildlife or natural features of the park, and at the time of Sheridan's visit, wildlife inside Yellowstone was managed essentially the same as it was outside. More importantly, most of the country around Yellowstone at that time remained in a natural condition, not because anyone was protecting it, but because there were few demands to exploit or develop the area. Where there was a marketable resource, it was difficult and expensive to extract. But in recent years these demands have escalated dramatically and now affect or threaten to affect large and sensitive areas. We are compelled to acknowledge that Yellowstone Park's living systems and thermal features may not survive intact unless large areas surrounding it are managed with the park's needs given priority.

Those concerned about the threats to Yellowstone from activities on adjacent federal, state and private lands would, of course, dearly love to re-draw the park boundaries to include within it those nearby areas upon which the environmental integrity of Yellowstone depends. Others more interested in logging, mining, oil and gas and geothermal exploration and production, roads, dams, recreational and second-home developments and myriad other interests doubtless also would like to re-draw Yellowstone's boundaries. But it is unlikely that the boundaries of Yellowstone National Park will change much. Some adjustments and additions to park lands, however, could occur as threats to the park become more imminent.

Taking the current ownership and administrative authority over these lands as a given, we must focus our attention on management of Greater Yellowstone as a region of concern, a biological community, an ecosystem, a geological thermal system. Whatever we might wish to call it, we must recognize that Yellowstone National Park is not an island, cut off and unrelated to adjacent lands. It is, rather, part of a much larger and highly interrelated "Greater Yellowstone" area.

How we define the geographic extent of Greater Yellowstone depends upon which of its characteristics we use as criteria for delineating boundaries. Were wildlife biologists to employ their criteria, they might take into account the

W. PERRY CONWAY

TOM MURPHY

entire community of wildlife centered in Yellowstone but ranging far beyond park boundaries. By this measure, an ecosystem includes all the elements required to perpetuate all the species indigenous to an area including a substantial amount of genetic exchange among populations of major vertebrates. It would also include the winter ranges for migrating mammals, which in some instances lie at considerable distances from the park itself but which are essential for the survival of healthy wildlife populations. It also might include the range for natural diffusion (as opposed to seasonal migration) from one part of the biological community to another. To a wildlife biologist, the outer boundaries of Greater Yellowstone could therefore be drawn at barriers to migration or diffusion. Such barriers might be man-made and include areas of concentrated human settlement, highways, major mining or logging operations, dams and reservoirs, or agricultural developments.

Geologists, on the other hand, might define Greater Yellowstone in terms of major geological formations or landforms, or might include large areas of geothermal resources that lie outside Yellowstone to the north, west and southwest. These boundaries would differ substantially from the rectangle that Congress established in 1872.

A third approach to defining Greater Yellowstone could employ hydrographic criteria and focus on Greater Yellowstone as an area that encompasses the headwaters of the rivers and streams that arise on the high bubble of earth known as the Yellowstone Plateau.

This high country in and immediately adja-

We stopped at this place and for my own part I almost wished I could spend the remainder of my days in a place like this where happiness and contentment seemed to reign in wild romantic splendor surrounded by majestic battlements which seemed to support the heavens and shut out all hostile intruders.

OSBORNE RUSSELL, 1835
IN *JOURNAL OF A
TRAPPER*

HENRY H. HOLDSWORTH

Left: *Stinkbug on sumac leaves tinted by autumn.*

Facing page: *Minerva Terrace at Mammoth Hot Springs, Yellowstone National Park.*

TOM MURPHY

Above: *Elk cows and calves.*

Facing page: *Castle Geyser.*

cent to Yellowstone National Park gives rise to every major river and stream within a radius of 100 miles. The Yellowstone, Gallatin and Madison rivers are born here, and the mountains of the park's eastern boundary give rise to the Clark's Fork of the Yellowstone, the Shoshone, and the Grey Bull rivers. All of these rivers flow east from the Continental Divide. It is also within the park proper where the Snake River begins its course west of the Continental Divide, first south into Jackson Hole then generally west to its confluence with the Columbia near Pasco in southeast Washington State.

Immediately west of the park boundary, the Henrys Fork flows south for miles through the Island Park region before dropping sharply off the rim of an ancient caldera into the farmlands of Idaho, where it joins the Snake. In the extreme southeastern reaches of this area, just 50 miles from the corner of the park, the Green River begins its long journey southward through Wyoming and Utah to its confluence with the Colorado in the canyon lands of the southwest. Across a high divide just a few miles northwest of the upper Green, the waters of the Gros Ventre River originate and flow off to join the Snake River in the middle of Jackson Hole.

While each of these approaches to defining Greater Yellowstone has merit, none of them alone possesses the precision, comprehensive scope and objectivity we desire. For this reason, I have opted to use the concepts of ecosystem and ecoregion developed by R. G. Bailey and A. W. Kuchler, and adopted by the U.S. Forest Service for use in its Roadless Area Review and Evaluation II (RARE II) studies during the late 1970s. Although a bit more complex than the other approaches described above, the ecosystem concept enables us to base definitions on observable properties and provides us with boundaries that encompass the wildlife communities and unique geological phenomena of this region.

Bailey and Kuchler describe an ecosystem as "any potential natural vegetation-type within an ecoregion." Potential vegetation is "vegetation that would exist today if man were removed from the scene and if the plant succession after his removal were telescoped into a single moment." (This should not be confused with the actual vegetation observed at the present.)

The map on page 64 shows the area of similar potential natural vegetation in the Greater Yellowstone area. Bailey's criteria for ecosystem classification according to potential natural vegetation clearly shows that there is an ecologi-

TOM MURPHY

cal community we can call Greater Yellowstone and that its boundaries generally coincide with boundaries that might be based on wildlife considerations. Wildlife, for example, depends on plants for food, and at times for shelter and breeding areas as well. Even where plants do not control wildlife distribution, they often indicate the kinds of climate and soil types upon which wildlife depends. From this it seems we can in fact talk of the "Greater Yellowstone Ecosystem" as an ecological entity with fairly well defined boundaries.

The map on page 65 delineates the boundaries of the Greater Yellowstone ecosystem as we will define them in this book.

While the concept of potential natural vegetation provides us with a definition of the Greater Yellowstone Ecosystem, one needn't be a scientist to see the connections that tie Yellowstone Park to its surroundings. We said earlier that some of Yellowstone's wildlife species range far beyond the national park boundary and depend heavily on adjacent lands for survival. Two of Yellowstone's most famous inhabitants, the grizzly bear and elk, illustrate this point.

THE GRIZZLY BEAR: THE PARK IS NOT ENOUGH

It is estimated that in 1800 there were perhaps 100,000 grizzly bears roaming North America—today there are fewer than 1,000. The great bears in the Yellowstone area are a remnant population, tied to ever-diminishing wild lands. Grizzlies disappeared from Texas in 1890, passed from former abundance to extinction in California in 1922, were gone from Utah by 1923, Oregon by 1931, New Mexico by 1933, and Arizona by 1935. Today, only two areas remain in the entire lower 48 states where significant populations of grizzlies

Right: *View from space. Yellowstone Park and environs from 150 miles up. Park boundary is indicated by dotted line. The light orange area in the center of the park is the Hayden Valley. The three large lakes southwest of Yellowstone Lake are, from right to left, Shoshone, Lewis and Heart Lakes.*

The northern tip of Jackson Lake and a small part of the Teton Range can be seen at the extreme bottom center of the photo. Montana's Madison Range is at the extreme upper left. Hebgen and Quake Lakes are below and right of the Madison Range, and Henry's Lake lies below and left of Hebgen Lake. Note the extensive areas of clear cut logging which show as light green areas along Yellowstone's western boundary.

As this view from space indicates, the Yellowstone Park boundary bears no relationship to biological entities. Neither does it bear a relationship to geological or geographic considerations except along the east side of the park where a portion of the boundary line was modified early in this century to correspond to the crest of the Absaroka Mountain Range. (ERTS/LANDSAT satellite image courtesy of EROS Data Center, U.S. Geological Survey.)

Facing page: *The West Boulder River meadows, Absaroka-Beartooth Wilderness Area.*

TOM MURPHY

Algae growth around Morning Glory Pool.

SALVATORE J. VASPOL

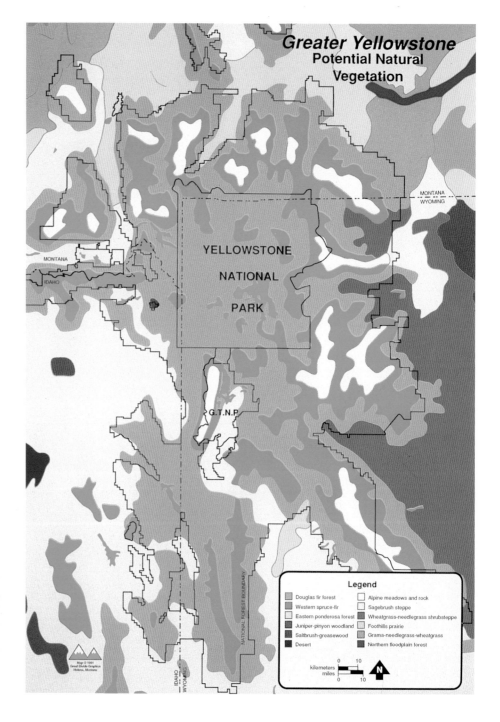

Greater Yellowstone
Potential Natural
Vegetation

MONTANA
WYOMING

MONTANA

IDAHO

YELLOWSTONE

NATIONAL

PARK

G.T.N.P.

NATIONAL FOREST BOUNDARY

IDAHO
WYOMING

Map © 1991
Great Divide Graphics
Helena, Montana

Legend

Douglas fir forest	Alpine meadows and rock
Western spruce-fir	Sagebrush steppe
Eastern ponderosa forest	Wheatgrass-needlegrass shrubsteppe
Juniper-pinyon woodland	Foothills prairie
Saltbrush-greasewood	Grama-needlegrass-wheatgrass
Desert	Northern floodplain forest

kilometers   0   10

miles   0   10

N

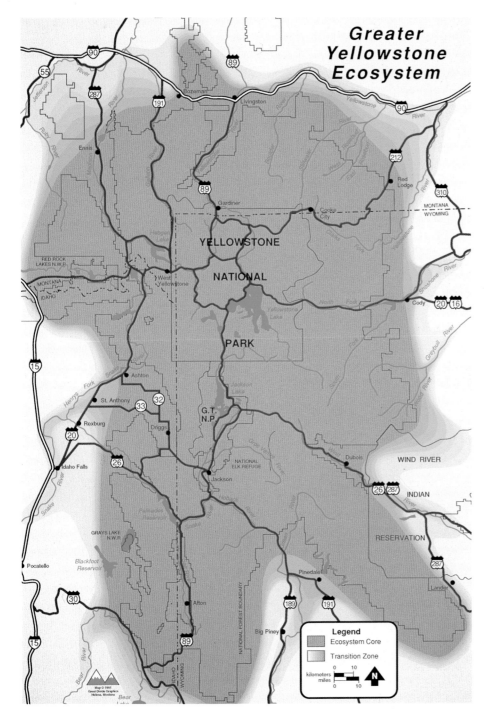

Greater Yellowstone Ecosystem

Legend

Ecosystem Core

Transition Zone

Osprey in nest, Grand Canyon of the Yellowstone River.

BARBARA & MICHAEL PFLAUM

RICK GRAETZ

Granite Peak in the Beartooth Mountains. **Facing page:** *Lonesome Lake and Mitchell Peak in the Wind River Range.*

survive. One is the Greater Yellowstone Ecosystem, the other is the area sometimes referred to as the Northern Continental Divide Ecosystem, which includes Glacier National Park and large areas of formally designated wilderness in the Bob Marshall, Great Bear, Scapegoat and Mission Mountain wilderness areas to the south of Glacier, and Canadian wild lands to the north.

Yellowstone National Park is what biologists call a grizzly population center, an area essential to the survival of the bear, and an area where the grizzly's activity under natural, free-ranging conditions is common. Habitat needed for the survival of the species is found here. Not surprisingly, however, the biological boundaries of the Yellowstone grizzly population center don't stop at the national park boundary—indeed, they reach far beyond the lands of the park. By even the most conservative estimates, 2 to 3 million acres of the population center lie outside the park. At the bare minimum, more than 40 percent of the essential habitat of Yellowstone grizzly bears lies beyond the park, and the distribution of grizzly bears is not limited only to population centers. In 1979, the U.S. Fish and Wildlife Service designated an area within the Greater Yellowstone ecosystem as occupied territory (map, page 68), a term that refers to an area in which confirmed grizzly bear sightings have occurred with some frequency in recent years. Yet even the area defined as occupied territory probably understates the distribution of the bear in the Greater Yellowstone area. The boundaries of occupied territory were defined through a series of compromises, some made on

DENNIS J. CWIDAK

The first fall on the Yellowstone, Hawkins and myself were coming up the river in search of camp, when we discovered a very large bar on the opposite bank. We shot across, and thought we had killed him, fur he laid quite still....we tied our mules and left our guns, clothes, and everything except our knives and belts, and swum over to whar the bar war. But instead of being dead, as we expected, he sprung up as we come near him, and took after us. Then you ought to have seen two naked men run! It war a race for life, and a close one, too. But we made the river first. The bank war about fifteen feet high above the water, and the river ten or twelve feet deep; but we didn't halt. Overboard we went, the bar after us....You can reckon that I swam! Every moment I felt myself being washed into the yawning jaws of the mighty beast, whose head war up the stream, and his eyes on me. But the current war too strong for him, and swept him along as fast as it did me....Hawkins war the first to make the shore, unknown to the bar, whose head war still up stream; and he set up such a whooping and yelling that the bar landed too, but on the opposite side. I made haste to follow Hawkins, who had landed on the side of the river we started from, either by design or good luck: and then we traveled back a mile and more to whar our mules war left...

JOE MEEK, AS TOLD TO
FRANCES VICTOR IN *THE
RIVER OF THE WEST*, 1870

MICHAEL H. FRANCIS

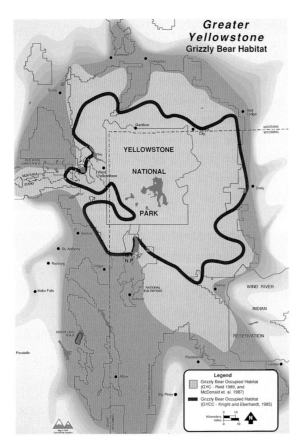

Greater
Yellowstone
Grizzly Bear Habitat

Legend

Grizzly Bear Occupied Habitat
(GYC - Reid 1989, and
McDonald et. al. 1987)

Grizzly Bear Occupied Habitat
(GYCC - Knight and Eberhardt, 1985)

that it encompasses a total area several times the size of the park itself. "It is blatantly clear," John Townsley, former superintendent of Yellowstone Park was quoted as saying in 1982, "that the grizzly bear cannot survive if Yellowstone National Park is its only refuge. It also needs portions of the five adjacent forests." A similar point is made by Dick Knight, leader of the Interagency Grizzly Bear Study Team, a group of bear researchers that has studied the Yellowstone grizzly for nearly 20 years, when he said, "Most grizzly bears cross state, forest and park boundaries several times a year, making populations within any political jurisdiction meaningless, and cooperative management a necessity." Clearly, for the bear—as for nearly every other species and ecological relationship—Yellowstone Park is not an island.

But while Yellowstone National Park is not an island for the grizzly bear, the Greater Yellowstone ecosystem is. As the map on this page demonstrates, there is no corridor for bears to move from Greater Yellowstone to another area of suitable bear habitat outside this ecosystem. By contrast, the Glacier Park grizzly is far better able to move long distances over contiguous areas of good habitat throughout the Bob Marshall complex to the south, and to the north far into Canada. But the Yellowstone grizzly is, in essence, trapped in Greater Yellowstone—if it is to live at all, all of its needs, including areas safe from man, must be met here. There is nowhere else to go.

Approximately 4,000 elk inhabit the southern reaches of Yellowstone National Park during the summer and fall months. Since this portion of the park does not constitute a complete ecological unit in which the elk can survive year round, the herd migrates south out of the park to lower elevations and suitable winter range. With the destruction of their historic winter range (caused

the basis of political considerations. They should be seen as fuzzy lines, miles thick and encompassing a considerably larger area than the map portrays.

Under the provisions of the Endangered Species Act of 1973, when a species is listed as threatened or endangered (the grizzly was listed as threatened in 1975), the U.S. Fish and Wildlife Service is supposed to designate critical habitat as a "means whereby the ecosystem upon which endangered species depend, may be considered, protected or restored." The critical habitat proposed by the agency in the mid-1970s was considerably larger than occupied territory as it is currently defined.

We needn't argue about how far beyond the boundaries of Yellowstone National Park the home of the grizzly bear extends, so long as we recognize

GEORGE WUERTHNER

Permanent grizzly ranges and permanent wilderness areas are of course two names for one problem. Enthusiasm about either requires a long view of conservation, and a historical perspective. Only those able to see the pageant of evolution can be expected to value its theater, the wilderness, or its outstanding achievement, the grizzly. But if education really educates, there will, in time, be more and more citizens who understand that relics of the old West add meaning and value to the new. Youth yet unborn will pole up the Missouri with Lewis and Clark, or climb the Sierras with James Capen Adams, and each generation in turn will ask: Where is the big white bear? It will be a sorry answer to say he went under while conservationists weren't looking.

ALDO LEOPOLD,
A SAND COUNTY
ALMANAC, 1948

Left: *Headwaters of Granite Creek in the Gros Ventre Wilderness Area, Wyoming.*

Facing page: *Grizzly bear.*

THE BALD EAGLE: FEARSOME RAPTOR WITH A FRAGILE POPULATION

There are approximately 200 bald eagles in the Greater Yellowstone ecosystem, including several dozen breeding pairs. Prior to 1960, a precipitous decline in the eagle population occurred here, due largely to the indiscriminate use of DDT. By the early 1970s when DDT finally was banned, both the Yellowstone Park population unit and the unit inhabiting the upper Madison River, Red Rocks, and the Henrys Fork River had been decimated. Only along the Snake River in Jackson Hole, where DDT had not been sprayed, did the eagle population remain stable.

While the eagle population in Greater Yellowstone has recovered, the Yellowstone Park population remains fragile. Most of the park is still covered by snow and its lakes are frozen during the nesting months of March and April. In some years, the entire Yellowstone Park eagle unit may not produce a single new eagle. In a good year, perhaps half a dozen may be raised.

This means that the Yellowstone Park unit must depend heavily upon an influx of eagles from Jackson Hole and the Upper Henrys Fork–Red Rocks–Upper Madison unit. Unless eagle habitat in those areas is carefully protected, there can be no influx of eagles into Yellowstone Park, and without that, Yellowstone's eagles probably would decline in number dramatically and perhaps even disappear.

DIANA STRATTON

THE TRUMPETER SWAN: SUCCESS STORY ON THE WING

No one knows how many trumpeter swans used to inhabit North America—perhaps a hundred thousand, perhaps many times that number. But in 1932, there were believed to be only 69 in the lower 48 states. Two thirds of the survivors were in a single spot, the Centennial Valley and Red Rocks Lake in southern Montana; the rest were in Yellowstone Park a few miles to the east. There may also have been a tiny remnant somewhere in Canada, but for all practical purposes, the Greater Yellowstone Ecosystem was the only spot left for this splendid bird, a creature weighing more than 20 pounds and exhibiting a wing span of eight feet. Greater Yellowstone was the trumpeter's final chance, the last place on earth where it could make it.

With the increased protection provided by establishment of the Red Rocks National Wildlife Refuge in 1935, in conjunction with other conservation measures, the outlook for the swan improved. Within 15 years their numbers at Red Rocks and nearby areas climbed to 300. Today the North American population of the magnificent trumpeter numbers about 10,000 and is frequently seen on the cold, clear streams, lakes and ponds of Yellowstone.

But even now, serious problems may lie ahead for the trumpeter in Greater Yellowstone, where its numbers have declined dramatically in the past two decades. A September, 1986 count of the swans found only 366 in the Greater Yellowstone ("tri-state") population. Scientists do not understand the complex causes of this decline, but most agree that survival of this magnificent bird in the Greater Yellowstone Ecosystem is threatened.

The fact that most of the surviving swans in 1932 were outside the boundaries of Yellowstone National Park itself is yet another example of why the larger area we call Greater Yellowstone is so important to wild land preservation, and why it is so important for the Greater Yellowstone Ecosystem to survive intact.

DIANA STRATTON

primarily by human settlement and agricultural development), many of the elk now concentrate at the National Elk Refuge in Jackson, Wyoming where they are fed pellets and hay to make it through the winter. Without the refuge or without migration corridors to reach it, some of the southern Yellowstone elk would perish. They too have no place else to go.

In addition to the southern Yellowstone elk herd, other major herds migrate to non-park lands for winter range, as shown by the map on page 72. The park's largest collection of elk, known as the northern Yellowstone elk herd, summers across nearly two thirds of Yellowstone Park, but moves north into the lower valleys of the Lamar and Yellowstone rivers as winter approaches. During periods of the deepest snowfall, about 15 percent of the northern herd's animals, will migrate down the Yellowstone River out of the park and into Montana where they winter on state, private and national forest lands. In the northwest corner of the park, the Gallatin elk herd travels as many as 20 miles into the Gallatin Canyon of southwestern Montana. And near the southwestern corner of the park a smaller herd migrates out of the Bechler River area across the Targhee National Forest of Idaho to winter range on the Sand Creek Desert more than 25 miles beyond the park boundary. Other herds move out of the park to the east and southeast crossing onto the North Absaroka and Washakie wilderness areas and adjacent lands. Such migrations, of course, are not limited to elk; other wildlife species such as pronghorn, deer, bighorn sheep and a variety of birds and fish also move back and forth across national park, national forest, state and private lands in Montana, Wyoming and Idaho.

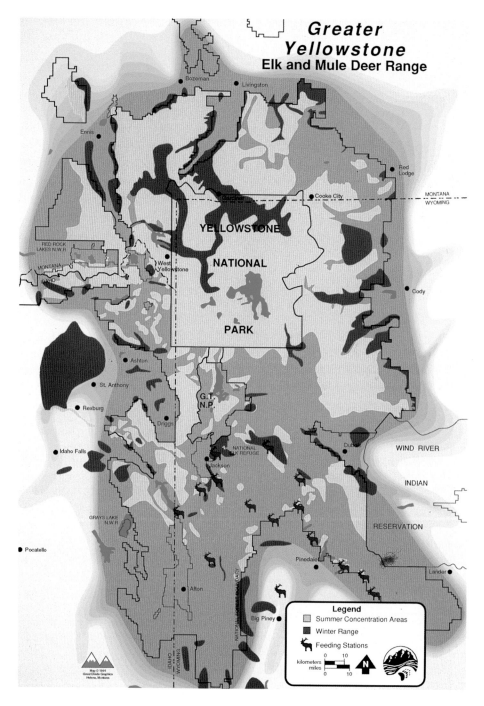

Greater Yellowstone
Elk and Mule Deer Range

Legend
- Summer Concentration Areas
- Winter Range
- Feeding Stations

kilometers
miles

Map © 1991
Great Divide Graphics
Helena, Montana

GREATER YELLOWSTONE UNDERGROUND

As we consider the relationship between Yellowstone National Park and the surrounding lands, it becomes increasingly clear that we must take into account geological as well as ecological factors. The fabulous thermal areas of the park might be connected by subsurface systems to areas beyond the park boundary to the southwest and north. Commercial geothermal exploration and development have been proposed immediately adjacent to the southwest park boundary in an area known as the Island Park Geothermal Area.

Concern about such development so close to Yellowstone Park focuses on the question of what effect drilling there may have on the park's geysers, the rarest and most fragile of geothermal phenomena. In 1979 an elaborate environmental impact statement prepared by the U.S. Forest Service to consider the issue concluded: "The exact boundaries of the Yellowstone geothermal reservoir or reservoirs are uncertain, and no definite evidence is apparently available on what the permeability is at depth. Thus it is hard to say how much of a connection, if any, there is between the possible geothermal resource of the Island Park Geothermal Area and thermal areas inside the park, or if any adverse effects might result."

Another area of interest to geothermal developers lies just north of the park boundary in the Corwin Springs Known Geothermal Resource Area. It is highly probable that the thermal systems of Yellowstone and the Corwin Springs geothermal area are connected and drilling here could threaten Mammoth Hot Springs and its incomparable travertine terraces just four miles to the south.

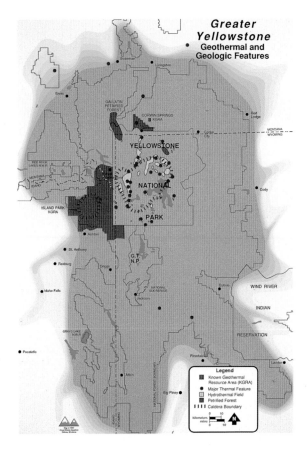

THE POLITICAL FRAGMENTATION OF GREATER YELLOWSTONE

In sharp contrast to the ecological (and possibly geological) relationships that tie the lands of Greater Yellowstone into one cohesive region, political and administrative boundaries untie the area and break it into myriad smaller unrelated jurisdictions (see map, page 93). The millions of acres of national forest lands surrounding Yellowstone National Park lie on seven different national forests, each with its own forest supervisor and separate administrative staff. Two of these forest supervisors (Targhee and Bridger-Teton) answer

The true test of the nature of national character is in what people choose, by a conscious act, in the face of contending choices, to preserve.

ROBIN W. WINKS,
CHAIRMAN
NATIONAL PARK SERVICE
ADVISORY BOARD

ALAN & SANDY CAREY

Above: *Flyfishing in the blue-ribbon Yellowstone River.*

Right: *Alpine forget-me-not.*

Facing page: *Bison drying off after crossing the Yellowstone River.*

JEFF FOOTT

to a Forest Service regional office in Ogden, Utah; one (Shoshone) answers to an office in Denver, Colorado; and two (Gallatin and Custer) to an office in Missoula, Montana. Three wildlife refuges, the National Elk Refuge in Jackson, Wyoming near the southern end of Greater Yellowstone, and Red Rocks National Wildlife Refuge near the western extent of Greater Yellowstone, are run by different managers who answer to a regional office in Denver.

Although most of Yellowstone National Park itself is in Wyoming, small portions are in Idaho and Montana. Three park entrances—West Yellowstone, Gardiner and Cooke City—are in Montana, while the east and south entrances are in Wyoming. The Greater Yellowstone Ecosystem spreads far into all three states and into portions of 10 counties. Yellowstone and Grand Teton national parks have separate superintendents and administrative staffs. Yellowstone has exclusive federal jurisdiction (being created as a park long before Wyoming, Idaho or Montana became states), but park officials in Grand Teton must share jurisdiction with the Wyoming Game and Fish Department, Teton County, the Wyoming Highway Patrol, a local airport board and others. Add this geographical, political and administrative fragmentation to the dramatically differing mission charged to each of these agencies, and one begins to appreciate why the Greater Yellowstone area has never been managed as an ecological unit. That does not mean there is no cooperation among the various agencies; the Cooperative Elk Management Group and the Interagency Grizzly Bear Study Team are examples of long-standing, joint-management undertakings. In very recent years, the Forest Service and the National Park Service have moved ahead in their "Aggregation" and "Vision" projects under the auspices of the joint Greater Yellowstone Coordinating Committee. But in other instances cooperation between agencies is still lacking, leading to piecemeal administrative decisions with little consideration given to the Greater Yellowstone area as a whole.

Greater Yellowstone, then, is an enormous area of wild lands comprising America's largest essentially intact ecosystem existing outside Alaska; it is surely one of the largest such temperate-zone ecosystem remaining anywhere on earth. More than 75 percent of the entire area is public land entrusted to the stewardship of federal agencies but belonging to all Americans and of interest to the people of the world. Will that stewardship be exercised wisely and in a manner that will retain intact the biological communities of the ecosystem? Will it continue to supply the arid west with abundant pure water, protect forever the environmental integrity of Yellowstone National Park, and maintain a meaningful piece of America's wild-land heritage for the people of the third millenium and beyond? The American people must decide.

"A thousand Yellowstone wonders are calling,
'Look up and down and round about you!'"
JOHN MUIR, 1898
WEST YELLOWSTONE

W. PERRY CONWAY

THE WOLF: MISSING LINK

The wolf once reigned as the master predator of Yellowstone's large hoofed animals, but today it is gone from Yellowstone, the victim of a deliberate and highly successful extermination campaign. Beginning more than 100 years ago and continued for half a century, that campaign had the official sanction of the guardians of the park—the U.S. Army and later the National Park Service. The extermination campaign, which extended to mountain lions, coyotes and wolverines, was based on the mistaken notion that some animals are good and some are bad, with the ungulates—elk, deer, moose, pronghorn, bighorn sheep and bison—deemed good.

Appealing as such a notion may be to the uninformed, it can be a disaster to the ecological scheme of things. Wildlife biologists today know that predators are integral components of a biological balancing act that, when given a chance, functions well in nature.

While inside Yellowstone itself humans were protecting "good" ungulates from "bad" predators, outside the park livestock predation by wolves was the rationale for predator extermination. It is ironic that the reason for war on the wolf stemmed almost entirely from another biological misdeed, the decimation of the large herds of bison that were the wolf's primary food source. The simultaneous introduction of domestic livestock into wolf range sealed the predators' fate as they were forced to turn from a diminishing native prey base to cattle and sheep. By 1925, the wolf essentially had been erased from the western landscape, and Yellowstone National Park was no exception. Since 1973, the wolf has been classified as an endangered species in the west.

The war against "bad" animals in the west utilized traps, guns and poisons. Between 1915 and 1941, the federal government's Bureau of Biological Survey killed 24,000 wolves in the western United States. Yellowstone was one of the last strongholds of the creature, but even here the wolf was not safe. Between 1914 and 1926, at least 136 wolves were killed in the park. The natural process of thinning ungulate populations (especially elk) through predation by wolves upon the sick, old, weak, unwary—and occasionally upon healthy—animals had been short-circuited.

Many biologists believe that there are unnaturally high populations of elk in Yellowstone, although some Park Service researchers disagree. In a place where the forces of nature are left to operate without human interference, every piece in the ecological puzzle is needed. To be sure, the primary elk population regulator in Yellowstone National Park is winter kill, but the supplementary effect of wolf predation also may have been significant. Starvation of thousands of southern Yellowstone elk is prevented only by the intervention of feeding them hay at the National Elk Refuge at Jackson, Wyoming, and some researchers believe that native range in and near Yellowstone frequently is overgrazed by artificially large populations of elk. In areas outside Yellowstone, hunting mitigates some of the population pressures caused by lack of natural predation, but inside the park, where hunting is not allowed, the wolf is more sorely missed for whatever degree of elk predation it could provide.

One of the stated purposes of the National Park Service is to "conserve, perpetuate, and portray as a composite whole the indigenous…terrestrial fauna." Human intervention has taken the wolf from Yellowstone; perhaps it is time for us to return the wolf to a small fragment of its native habitat in Yellowstone National Park.

In 1980, the U.S. Fish and Wildlife Service approved a plan of the Northern Rocky Mountain Wolf Recovery Team to reestablish and maintain at least two viable populations of wolves in the northern Rocky Mountains. Given the needs of the wolf (most notably a year-round prey base, denning and rendezvous sites, and large areas of wild lands with minimal exposure to humans), the team was able to identify only three geographic areas that could provide everything necessary for wolf recovery. One was Glacier National Park and the large system of wildlands stretching south along the Continental Divide into Montana; a second was in central Idaho and centered on the River of No Return, Selway-Bitterroot, and Gospel-Hump Wilderness areas; the third, and probably the most promising, was the Greater Yellowstone area.

While it appears that most wildlife biologists who have considered the matter strongly favor establishment of a wolf population in Greater

Yellowstone, some vexing considerations have to be overcome before a viable wolf population once again will roam this country. One of these problems is socio-political rather than biological. To an American public brought up on the Three Little Pigs and Little Red Riding Hood, the wolf may not seem quite worthy of special favors (even though there is not a single documented case of an attack upon a human being by a healthy wolf in the entire history of the western United States). Livestock operators near Yellowstone are not enthusiastic about the return of the wolf either, yet strong support for the wolf is present in many quarters as the American public becomes better informed about the natural role of predation and of predators. In the last five years, public support for wolf re-introduction has soared and it now appears just a matter of time before some re-introduction measures are implemented.

Once the political climate is conducive for wolf recovery, the capture and transplanting of family units of wild wolves will be a difficult process. The Wolf Recovery Team has given much thought to how the wolves would be managed once transplanted. Their strategy is based on a zone system in which wolves straying beyond certain areas would be captured or killed. In Zone I, probably limited to Yellowstone National Park and some nearby national forest lands, the wolf would be protected. Its habitat would be maintained and resource management decisions would favor the needs of the wolf. Zone II would serve as a buffer zone and travel corridor and would have some key habitat components, but not enough to sustain a viable wolf population. This area would include additional national forest lands around Yellowstone and supporting the wolf would be considered as an important use, but not the primary use of the area. Wolf activity and its needs would be accommodated here, but not to the extent that they would preclude other high-priority land uses. Problem wolves would be controlled. Zone III would include areas beyond the corridor zone in which established human activities, such as livestock grazing, occur at a sufficient level to render wolf presence undesirable. The wolf would receive no extraordinary protection here, and conflicts with livestock and humans would be resolved against the wolf.

The biological case for returning the wolf to its former range in Greater Yellowstone is persuasive, but when the decision is made to go ahead with the reestablishment, it will be made only partly on biological grounds; political considerations will be at least as important.

Regardless of the merits of wolf reestablishment and its prospects for Greater Yellowstone, the fact that there is still a place left in the continental United States that meets the qualitative and quantitative wild land requirements of a wolf population, bespeaks again the extraordinary significance of this area. The wolf is gone, but its home remains essentially intact, ready for its return when the time comes.

CHARLES KAY

ALAN & SANDY CAREY

Hoarfrost artistry in Yellowstone National Park. **Facing page:** *Yellow warbler.*

THREATS TO
GREATER YELLOWSTONE

In May 1980, the Office of Science and Technology of the National Park Service completed the first comprehensive survey identifying threats to the natural and cultural resources of America's national parks. The report was prepared during the last months of the Carter Administration. Interior Secretary James Watt and other officials of the Reagan Administration were not enthusiastic about it.

The report's findings are sobering and suggest a bleak future for many of our park lands. In terms of the total number of threats identified per park, Yellowstone ranked eighth among 310 national parks, monuments, and other units of the national park system. Perhaps more significantly, of the 12 parks in the United States that have been designated Biosphere Reserves by UNESCO in recognition of their global importance as representative ecosystems and irreplaceable genetic resources, Yellowstone is the second most threatened, exceeded only by Glacier Na-

JEFF FOOTT

tional Park. As a group, these Biosphere Reserve parks, some of America's choicest ecosystems, average three times as many threats per park as non-biosphere reserve areas. Clearly, size, remoteness and fame are no guarantee against degradation.

"Without qualifications," the report said, "it can be stated that the cultural and natural resources of the parks are endangered both from without and from within by a broad range of such threats....These threats which emanate from both internal and external forces are causing severe degradation of park resources."

Clearly, all is not well with America's national parks, as indicated in the bleak conclusion of the State of the Parks Report: "There is no question that these threats will continue to degrade and destroy irreplaceable park resources until such time as mitigation measures are implemented. In many cases this degradation or loss of resources is irreversible. It represents a sacrifice by the public that, for the most part, is unaware that such a price is being paid."

BILL & BOBBIE ASHER

Near the top of the list of those areas most threatened sits Yellowstone. The park and the Greater Yellowstone Ecosystem are inextricably linked. As the heart of that ecosystem, Yellowstone National Park cannot possibly survive unimpaired if the ecological unit of Greater Yellowstone is allowed to disintegrate. What is good for the Greater Yellowstone Ecosystem will be good for Yellowstone National Park.

The types of activities that threaten to disrupt the Greater Yellowstone Ecosystem vary widely. The threats inventory compiled for Yellowstone in the State of the Parks report identified 67 specific kinds of threats that were deemed harmful or probably harmful to Yellowstone—43 of the 67 were classified as threats originating partly or entirely outside Yellowstone's boundaries. Of these external threats, those posing the greatest potential for large-scale disruption included oil and gas exploration and development, logging, mining, geothermal energy development, hydropower and reclamation projects, and resorts, subdivisions and recreational developments. Others, such as poor grazing practices, use of poisons and herbicides, power lines, overuse by humans, water pollution, and a series of political schemes to sell public lands and provide greater motor vehicle access to back-country areas pose smaller threats that may nonetheless be highly significant.

The impact of these threats taken one at a time could be mitigated, but taken collectively, and in the absence of some immediate protective measures, their cumulative effect threatens to disrupt this system of wild lands to such degree that an irreversible degradation of the biological and geological communities of the Greater Yellowstone Ecosystem and Yellowstone National Park seems inescapable. A closer look at the nature of those activities and developments that are now occurring in Greater Yellowstone will help us understand why they forebode such large-scale degradation.

OIL AND GAS EXPLORATION AND DEVELOPMENT

Large areas of the Greater Yellowstone Ecosystem include geological formations that many geologists believe are promising sites for the production of oil and gas. Parts of the western portion of the ecosystem lie within the so-called overthrust belt, folded and faulted slabs of rock that have been thrust over younger rocks creating traps that may contain oil and gas. Large discoveries of oil and gas have been made in the Canadian portion of the overthrust belt on the north

and in the Wyoming portion on the south, causing intense interest to focus on the area in between, including parts of Greater Yellowstone. Some of the eastern portion of the ecosystem is adjacent to areas of existing oil and gas activity. Geologists suspect that what they call the producing horizons of these areas lie under lands near the south and east boundaries of Yellowstone Park.

Oil and gas activity occurs in two major stages, exploration and subsequent development and production. During exploration a variety of geophysical investigations may be undertaken including mapping and gravitational, magnetic, and seismic prospecting. In remote back-country locations, seismic prospecting frequently has meant thousands of explosive charges detonating along seismic lines, heavy helicopter traffic and in-

Mr. Ingalls [John James Ingalls of Kansas]: The best thing that the Government could do with the Yellowstone National Park is to survey it and sell it as other public lands are sold.

Mr. Vest [George G. Vest of Missouri]: The last hope of the preservation of the bison, the buffalo, the moose, and the elk upon the continent of North America exists in the preservation of that park, and to such an extent that it will be a great preserve…I am not ashamed to say that I shall vote to perpetuate this park to the American people. I am not ashamed to say that I think its existence answers a great purpose in our national life. There should be to a nation that will have a hundred million or a hundred and fifty million people a park like this as a great breathing-place for the national lungs…

DEBATE IN THE
UNITED STATES SENATE,
MARCH 1, 1883

RICK GRAETZ

Left: Madison Mountain Range in the Lee Metcalf Wilderness.

Facing page: One cautious mule deer fawn.

Mr. McAdoo [William McAdoo of New Jersey]: A land famine is approaching. Our population from natural causes and a tremendous wave of immigration is rapidly increasing...Here is a great wonderland to be preserved for the benefit of our people, for that innumerable caravan that every year go out to see in the great West the inspiring sights and mysteries of nature that elevate mankind and bring it into closer communion with omniscience; I believe this park should be preserved upon this, if for no other ground. The glory of this territory is its sublime solitude. Civilization is becoming so universal that man can only see nature in her majesty and primal glory, as it were, in these as yet virgin regions.

DEBATE IN THE UNITED
STATES HOUSE OF
REPRESENTATIVES,
DECEMBER 14, 1886

U.S. FOREST SERVICE PHOTOS

Above left: *Helicopter working with seismic crews in search of oil and gas on the Bridger-Teton National Forest. Ninety-five percent of non-wilderness lands on the Bridger-Teton remain open to oil and gas leasing.* **Right:** *Exploratory drilling on the Bridger-Teton.*

Facing page: *Montana's Paradise Valley, just north of Yellowstone National Park.*

creased human presence, all of which tend to disturb and sometimes displace wildlife populations. This is especially true in areas of high geophysical interest, where criss-crossing and parallel seismic lines are shot across the same area over and over. Because findings are not shared among competing companies, each must do its own investigation, even though the same area may have been tested repeatedly by others.

In areas where an operator has a lease and where preliminary exploration shows promise, exploratory drilling may be conducted. This usually means road construction, heavy truck traffic, leveling and clearing of drill sites, and possibly mud pits, camps, buildings and more people. If oil or gas is discovered, the area is then developed for production.

The activities associated with oil and gas development and production are of large magnitude. More and larger roads are constructed, and pipelines, utility lines, separators, generators and storage tanks are built. Systems for pressure maintenance, waste disposal, recovery and communications are brought into the area along with more people and the elaborate support systems they require.

The environmental impact of such activities on wild lands can be devastating. A glimpse of how extensive these impacts may be is offered in a 1981 draft environmental impact statement on the proposed leasing of the Washakie Wilderness Area, which abuts a portion of the Yellowstone Park boundary on the east. In a section entitled "Summary of Adverse Impacts Which Cannot Be Avoided," the report predicted reduced wildlife winter range, declining populations of elk, moose, bighorn sheep (possibly below viable populations) and large predators, and reduced wildlife habitat and displacement of many wildlife species. Other impacts mentioned included soil erosion, water pollution, loss of recreational opportunities, more traffic and increased motorized trespass on newly

PAUL DIX

constructed roads. In a separate document dated September 14, 1981, Shoshone National Forest officials stated: "Oil and gas leasing [in Situation I bear areas] with its associated construction activities will have an adverse impact on the essential habitat and continued existence of the grizzly bear."

John Townsley, then superintendent of Yellowstone National Park, said of the proposal to lease the Washakie Wilderness: "The long term effects created by the impact of energy development would be devastating to the critical wildlife habitat and destroy the wilderness value in this wild, remote and incredibly scenic area adjoining Yellowstone National Park."

Once we understand the potential consequences of oil and gas development on the wild lands of Greater Yellowstone, we can begin to appreciate the magnitude of the problem. When this book was written in 1983, there were already 1,600 oil and gas leases on 2.3 million acres of the Bridger-Teton National Forest; 75 percent of the entire Targhee National Forest was leased or under lease application; half a million acres of the Washakie Wilderness was under lease application; 45,000 acres of the Gros Ventre Wilderness had been leased; 20,000 acres of the Absaroka-Beartooth Wilderness were under lease application; extensive areas of the Gallatin National Forest adjacent to Yellowstone National Park were under lease or lease application including 25,000 acres of essential grizzly bear habitat immediately adjacent to the Yellowstone Park boundary; and there were numerous applications for areas wholly or partially within designated wilderness areas on the Shoshone National Forest. Amoco, Arco, Chevron, Shell, Mobil, Getty, Exxon, and nearly every other major oil company in the country were involved. Today, thousands of leases and applications extend across millions of acres of the Greater Yellowstone Ecosystem.

In the early 1980s, under pressure from then-secretary of the Interior James Watt, it seemed that even congressionally-designated wilderness areas would be leased, explored and possibly drilled, but in 1982 Congress stepped in to prevent oil and gas development in wilderness and in areas recommended for wilderness during the RARE II process. Initially, the measure provided only interim protection, but it was extended to stop leasing until the permanent ban, written into the Wilderness Act in 1964, became effective on January 1, 1984. The wilderness leasing issue came to the fore in 1980 when the Department of Interior asked the Shoshone National Forest to consider granting 72 lease applications pending at that time in the Washakie Wilderness. From the outset it was clear that the law allowed such leasing in wilderness even though it was unprecedented. Conservationists called it a legal loophole, but the Forest Service recommended that 92,000 acres of the Washakie be open to oil and gas leasing and that 88 percent of the entire wilderness be open to geophysical exploration. The prospect of such leasing and the precedent it would set caused a storm of protest. This was the issue that led to my conversations (see Preface to the Second Edition) with John Townsley in 1981.

The congressional ban protects wilderness areas adjacent to Yellowstone National Park as well as some areas officially recommended for wilderness designation, but it does nothing about millions of acres of non-wilderness, or about those leases already granted in wilderness or recommended wilderness. The Gros Ventre Wilderness, southeast of Jackson Hole, Wyoming, was the largest single area in the lower 48 to be recommended for wilderness during the RARE II pro-

TOM MURPHY

cess. Wilderness designation for this extraordinary area was supported by 82 percent of those commenting during RARE II. Both the governor of Wyoming and the state Fish and Game Department supported wilderness here. Yet oil and gas leases are already granted on 45,000 acres of the Gros Ventre and it is not simply the direct and predictable impacts of oil and gas development that threaten this area; the unintended impact of deep drilling could be the affecting of geothermal resources in the area, including those of Yellowstone Park. In a recent memo, Irving Friedman, USGS research geochemist, pointed to this hazard when he said "Gas and oil development represents a threat to the features of [Yellowstone] Park at least as important as geothermal heat extraction."

Outside of those areas covered by the congressional ban, nearly every acre of Greater Yellowstone that can be leased is leased, some of it in sensitive areas. For the moment, no one knows if significant amounts of oil and gas will be found in the Greater Yellowstone Ecosystem, but if they are, everything is in place for development on grand scale.

GEOTHERMAL ENERGY DEVELOPMENT

Visitors to Yellowstone who take the time to attend an evening naturalist talk will learn that there is a great bubble of magma and hot rock underlying Yellowstone Park that provides the heat source to drive the park's unique thermal features. But what one might not be aware of is that other areas outside the park may also be underlain by hot rock, which is of great interest to geologists and to those who discern a potential for geothermal energy development.

There are three areas of particular interest that geologists call Known Geothermal Resource Areas (KGRA): two, the Yellowstone KGRA and the Island Park KGRA, lie along the west and southwest boundary of Yellowstone; a third, the Corwin Springs KGRA, is adjacent to the north park boundary near Gardiner, Montana. (See map page 73.) The relationship between the thermal features of Yellowstone and the nearby KGRA's outside the park are not well understood. It is suspected that these areas share a similar geologic history with Yellowstone, but unlike parts of Yellowstone where semi-molten magma lies relatively near the earth's surface, the KGRA's probably derive their thermal properties from residual heat in solid, but still hot, rock.

The Geothermal Steam Act of 1970 authorizes the leasing of national forest lands for geothermal exploration and development. In the Island Park Geothermal Area alone, more than 70 industrial and utility companies have applied for geothermal leases on some 77,000 acres of the Targhee National Forest. Leases already have been granted on 25,000 acres of state and private lands in the area. In response to this interest by energy developers, the U.S. Forest Service began an environmental impact study in 1975 to assess what geothermal development would mean for national forest land in the Yellowstone and Island Park KGRA's. In 1980 the Forest Service concluded that 37 percent of the Island Park Geo-

HENRY H. HOLDSWORTH

Left: *White pelican.*

Facing page: *Lightning-shot clouds mask a full moon over Yellowstone Lake.*

I don't consider Yellowstone Park as an island that can be self-perpetuated. All these activities in combination become a tremendous threat to Yellowstone.

JOHN TOWNSLEY
SUPERINTENDENT OF
YELLOWSTONE NATIONAL
PARK, 1975—1982

thermal Area (IPGA) should be leased only if the Secretary of the Interior, in consultation with the Secretary of Agriculture, determined that there was a valuable geothermal resource there, that development of such a resource would not adversely affect the thermal features of Yellowstone National Park or the habitat of threatened or endangered wildlife species, and that air and water pollution would not affect other resource values of the area.

During the Environmental Impact Statement (EIS) process, concern focused immediately upon the danger that geothermal drilling at Island Park might affect the geysers and other thermal features of Yellowstone Park. The thermal features on upper Boundary Creek in Yellowstone National Park are only two miles from the IPGA; 13 other known thermal features are within 12 miles, and Old Faithful itself is only 13 miles distant. Concern is warranted—seven of the world's 10 major geyser basins have been destroyed or seriously damaged by geothermal exploration or development. In New Zealand, the Geyser Thermal Valley, which ranked fifth among the major geyser areas on earth, died shortly after the Wairakei plant was installed nearby. In 1965 the last known geyser eruption occurred there, and in 1972 the Geyser Thermal Valley was closed as a tourist attraction. And the destruction of New Zealand's geyser fields has not been limited to the Geyser Thermal Valley. The December 1982 newsletter of the New Zealand Geochemical Group reported that "There was a time when New Zealand had 130 geysers but now it has only five…" The article also documented destruction of Papakura Geyser in 1975, and the final demise of Malfroy Geyser "immediately after drills were placed…"

The destruction of geysers by geothermal

JEFF VANUGA

drilling has not been limited to New Zealand. As the Island Park EIS notes, near cessation or total destruction of natural hot springs or geyser activity has occurred in Iceland, Italy and Nevada. The Beowawe Geysers of Nevada were second only to those of Yellowstone on the North American continent prior to geothermal exploration from 1945 to 1958. During that period wells were drilled, and by 1961 all springs and geysers had ceased flowing. The geysers of Steamboat Springs, Nevada were similarly destroyed by the early 1960s.

It is important to note that although thermal areas are not particularly unusual, geysers are extremely rare and are the most fragile of all geothermal phenomena. They require the occurrence of a highly unusual combination of factors and are easily disrupted. The case for extreme caution in Yellowstone is strong. It holds the greatest concentration

Right: *Mule deer buck.*

Facing page: *Aerial view of the aptly-named Prismatic Pool, Yellowstone National Park.*

of geysers in the world (there are more geysers here than on the rest of the earth combined) and it is probably the only major undisturbed geyser area left on earth.

It is simply not known if there is a connection between the thermal features of Yellowstone Park and the IPGA. America's best geologists are unwilling to guarantee that drilling in the IPGA will not affect the thermal features of Yellowstone. According to geologist Duncan Foley, a specialist in geothermal geology, "Anybody who says they have an absolute answer is overstating his case. Nobody agrees because nobody knows for sure."

Research in recent years, however, indicates a greater likelihood of a connection than previously thought. Studies by the University of California in the southwest corner of Yellowstone during the summer of 1983 show the possibility of a much deeper heat source than most scientists had suspected. These findings suggest the presence of a local hot-water reservoir originating in the southwestern portion of Yellowstone. Research by the United States Geothermal Survey in the same area shows a conducting layer at shallow depth, which is consistent with a hot-water aquifer that may extend into the IPGA. Both findings point to a likely connection between the thermal features inside Yellowstone and the Island Park area. Recent studies of the Corwin Springs Geothermal Area just north of the Yellowstone Park boundary near Gardiner, Montana also show highly probable connections between park thermal features and thermal areas immediately north of the park.

Largely as a result of the controversy surrounding Island Park, Congress took an interest in the matter. In 1983, a law was enacted to ban geothermal leasing in the IPGA until the Secretary of the Interior determined that exploration and development would not have "a foreseeably signif-

icant adverse affect on nationally significant geothermal features." Another provision of the bill singled out the IPGA for a two-year study to determine if drilling there would harm the thermal features of Yellowstone Park. To make such a determination in two years was ambitious indeed given the fact that some of the best minds in the field of geology have been unable to determine if a geothermal resource even exists in the IPGA. To date, scientists still do not understand the relationship between the IPGA and the thermal features of Yellowstone.

The 1983 law applied only to federal lands in the IPGA; private and state leases were not affected—neither were a number of other geothermal areas including the Corwin Springs Geothermal Area just north of Yellowstone. In 1988 Congress acted again, this time in response to a project by

Those sorts of political-scientific conundrums, allowed to continue, will eventually tear the Greater Yellowstone Ecosystem apart. There is so much we still don't know about it, and much we will never know. We all have our own ideas of how it's put together and where the rents must be mended, and some of us are right and some are wrong. But again, nobody is in charge. So I suggest we give it over to its best and highest use, and let it be a museum, a laboratory, a place to make a naturalist's eyes bug out of her head. And not just the park. Let them have the whole Greater Yellowstone Ecosystem.

GEOF O'GARA
IN *HIGH COUNTRY NEWS*

PAUL DIX

There is no geothermal development in the world within a geyser basin area that has been done without adverse effects on the geysers.

**ROBERT HERBST
ASSISTANT SECRETARY OF
THE INTERIOR, 1979**

TOM MURPHY PHOTOS

the Church Universal and Triumphant, in which church land developers drilled a 400-foot well near La Duke Hot Springs to utilize hot water for space heating. The law provided for a three-year ban on leasing while scientists attempt to further understand the link between the Corwin Springs Geothermal Area and geothermal features in Yellowstone Park.

Aside from its potential impact on Yellowstone's thermal features, geothermal development raises other concerns for Yellowstone Park and the Greater Yellowstone Ecosystem. During the geothermal exploration stage, test wells are drilled. This means the use of truck-mounted drill rigs and compressors or water trucks. They need roads, they need drill pads, they need generators and sump pits and mud tanks and people.

Nearly 20 percent of the IPGA is in important grizzly bear habitat and Dick Knight, leader of the Interagency Grizzly Bear Study Team, was

Right: *Playtime for an otter couple.*
Above: *Sunrise at Old Faithful.*

Facing page: *February frost among Yellowstone's geysers.*

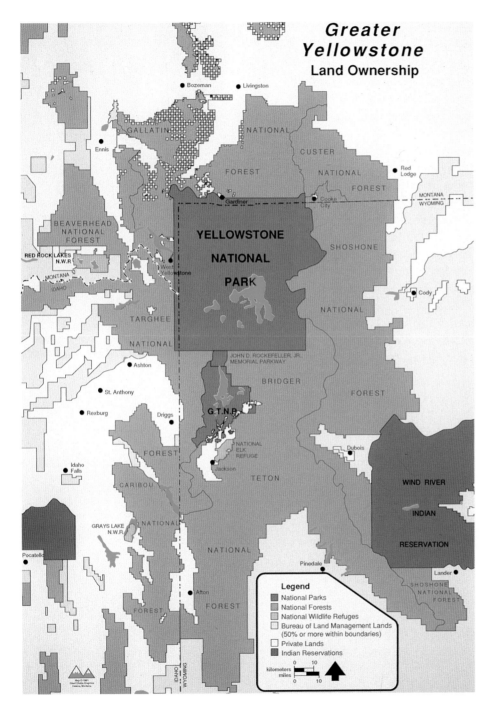

Greater Yellowstone
Land Ownership

Legend
- National Parks
- National Forests
- National Wildlife Refuges
- Bureau of Land Management Lands (50% or more within boundaries)
- Private Lands
- Indian Reservations

kilometers 0 10
miles 0 10

quoted more than 15 years ago as saying, "This geothermal development is the worst thing that can happen to the grizzly bear."

Fifty percent of the resident trumpeter swans winter within the IPGA; the endangered bald eagle and possibly the peregrine falcon find their homes here as do prairie falcons, ferruginous hawks, sharptail grouse, and possibly remnant populations of Canada lynx, fishers and wolverines. The open waters of the Henrys Fork River are, in the words of the U.S. Fish and Wildlife Service, "the primary wintering area of all of Canada's trumpeter swans." From a fisheries standpoint, the Henrys Fork itself is probably the most important stream in Idaho.

But perhaps most portentous of all is the prospect of well-mouth power plants and their enormous associated impacts that would come to the boundary of Yellowstone if an exploitable geothermal resource were found here. That could mean full-scale industrialization for the future of Island Park.

LOGGING

For years logging on the forests of the Greater Yellowstone Ecosystem was done on a relatively small scale by local operators. But with the arrival of large national and international wood products corporations in the area in the mid-1950s, cutting doubled, then doubled again by the mid-1960s. During this period enormous clearcuts were made on the forests of the west.

About half the national forest immediately adjacent to Yellowstone's boundary is in designated wilderness and therefore not available for timber sales. But the other half is not protected from logging and it is here that past, current and projected future logging practices are of concern. The

United States Forest Service is in the business of selling timber: the law provides that the government should be managing its forests on a sustained-yield basis; that is, it shouldn't allow cutting of more than is being replaced with new growth. But the pressure to cut more timber, even where the government loses money on the sale, has grown steadily. It costs the Forest Service more to cut timber in the Greater Yellowstone Ecosystem than the agency makes in timber sale revenue. These "deficit sales" cost the American taxpayer millions of dollars a year, yet they continue unabated. A recent study by Randall O'Toole, an Oregon resource economist, estimates that the Forest Service loses $11.56 for every tree it cuts in the region and subsidizes timber-related jobs at the rate of $13,000 per job per year.

In the Greater Yellowstone Ecosystem logging is of concern in several areas. Foremost among these is the Targhee National Forest which completely surrounds the southwest corner of Yellowstone National Park. (See satellite photo on page 62.) The largest timber sale ever made outside Alaska was made here on the Moose Creek Plateau adjacent to Yellowstone. The sale totalled 318 million board feet of timber, and when the last tree fell more than a hundred square miles of the area had been cut. (By comparison,

the nearby Gallatin National Forest in 1991 plans to cut about 21 million board feet per year.) Forest Service officials explain that much of the lodgepole pine on the Targhee near Yellowstone had been attacked by the pine beetle and was dead or dying and therefore needed to be cut to salvage it from loss.

Cutting the forests of Greater Yellowstone at the current pace and volume makes no sense. Economically it is a losing proposition; it is not sustainable environmentally; and when judged by a standard of "highest and best use" it does not measure up. There are simply better places than Greater Yellowstone to grow trees and harvest timber. It is too dry and too high, re-growth periods are too long and the quality of the timber is generally low. The forests of Greater Yellowstone have higher values in the form of wildlife habitat, watershed protection, recreation and scenery than they do in producing two-by-fours. This

TOM MURPHY

RICK GRAETZ

Right: Large logging clear cuts on the Gallatin National Forest along Yellowstone National Park's western boundary, with West Yellowstone, Montana visible beyond.
Above: Logging site right at the boundary of a roadless area proposed for addition to the Absaroka-Beartooth Wilderness.

Facing page: Morning fog lifting off Yellowstone National Park.

is especially true given the adverse effect that logging has on other resource values and the absurdity of deficit sale economics.

What does all this logging in the Greater Yellowstone area mean for Yellowstone National Park and the Greater Yellowstone Ecosystem? Several major impacts accompany logging operations in the slow-growth forests of the intermountain west. The most obvious and perhaps the most deleterious over the long run is the construction of roads into areas previously inaccessible by motor vehicles. Roads usually bring dramatically increased human presence that for many wildlife species can be disastrous. Cover, birthing areas, and other forms of sanctuary are lost. Migration routes often are disrupted, greater pressure occurs on wildlife to avoid humans, and hunting pressure increases. The net effect is frequently a decline in wildlife population. Displacement of the animals to other areas may occur if such areas are available, but as the cumulative pace of development in Greater Yellowstone accelerates, those neighboring areas already may be occupied by oil rigs, ski lifts, summer homes, motorcycles or mines. Roads can have other less obvious, but nonetheless serious, consequences. Soil and vegetation are disturbed, resulting in erosion and stream sedimentation, which are further compounded by skidding and timber removal once the logging operation itself begins.

Once the roads are in and the logs are out, the altered vegetative cover of the land becomes yet another concern. In many instances, the new vegetation in logged areas provides more abundant feed for wildlife than was available in the forested areas. This can be locally beneficial, but across an entire forest or region more sanctuary frequently is lost and more human pressure is gained to offset the benefit of short-term browse.

STAN OSOLINSKI

We need logs from our national forests. Whether we need the volume of logs we are taking from Greater Yellowstone at this time and in this place, next door to Yellowstone, and whether roads, sedimentation and poison are the best way to treat this land is a question that should be of interest to all concerned about the future of Greater Yellowstone.

MINING

In 1872 Congress passed a mining law that opened public domain lands to mineral prospecting and granted miners the right to claim minerals and the surface over such minerals for private purposes. In 1897 the law was broadened to include national forest lands.

So-called potential mining claims give the claimant full ownership and control of both minerals and the surface. This, in essence, converts public land to private property. For many decades claims were patented easily and the requirement that a claimant demonstrate a valuable mineral body on the claim was not monitored carefully or enforced by the government. Many of the private inholdings in today's wilderness areas, national parks and wildlife refuges were conveyed from the government to private parties as patented mining claims. Unpatented mining claims, on the other hand, grant only ownership of minerals, but not of the surface; surface ownership is retained by the government, and federal agencies have some say about how the surface resources are managed.

The 1872 mining law was passed at a time when mineral development and exploration was conducted primarily by individuals and small operators. It provided for the give-away of public minerals and public lands on a first-come basis. There was no competitive bidding for claimable

minerals, and there still isn't even today. Anyone can file an unpatented mining claim on national forest land. This right extends even to wilderness areas, which were open to claim until January 1, 1984. After that date no new claims would be granted in wilderness, but existing valid claims could be worked.

In recent years, the 1872 mining law has come under attack by conservation organizations that contend that it grants far too much latitude to miners at the expense of the public interest, especially on the national forests of the west. Under the law, anyone may stake a claim on national forest land; occupy and use the land for prospecting, mining and processing ore; clear timber on the claim and cut it for use in mining; barter, sell or mortgage their claim just as any other real property may be bought and sold. Perhaps most importantly the law grants access across

WAYNE SCHERR

DIANA STRATTON

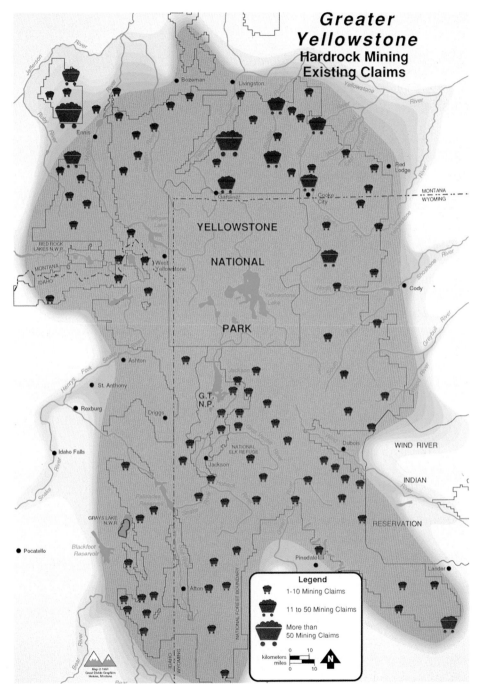

Greater Yellowstone
Hardrock Mining Existing Claims

Legend

1-10 Mining Claims

11 to 50 Mining Claims

More than 50 Mining Claims

kilometers 0 — 10
miles 0 — 10

N

Map © 1991 Great Divide Graphics Helena, Montana

other public lands when it is necessary to reach a claim on the national forest. For this the claimant pays the government nothing.

The law does require that a miner do a minimum of $100 per year worth of "assessment work" to maintain a valid claim, and also requires a miner to show that there is some valuable mineral or a good prospect of finding a valuable mineral on the claim. In practice, this last requirement is rarely enforced because the Forest Service has only a few mineral specialists to inspect thousands of claims. The Forest Service does, however, have the authority to require miners to conduct their operations in a manner that will minimize damage to the national forest, but such conditions may not "materially interfere" with the prospector's operations.

Mining claims, patented and unpatented, cover a large area of Greater Yellowstone. The greatest concentration of claims is clustered around the northeast corner of the park, throughout the Shoshone National Forest east of the park, and on the southeast, inside and adjacent to the Washakie Wilderness Area. The Forest Service estimates there are more than 2,300 mining claims in the North Absaroka and Washakie wildernesses and 380 claims in the Absaroka-Beartooth Wilderness. Most of these claims are not being worked at present, but higher metal prices could quickly fuel a mining boom in the area.

In the seven years since this book first was published, mining activity in the Greater Yellow-

Facing page, top: *Mining roads criss-cross the Absaroka Mountains.*
Bottom: *Bull elk crosses the Madison River during the 1988 fires in Yellowstone National Park.*

Mr. Toole [Joseph K. Toole of Montana Territory]: Mr. Chairman...I undertake to say that the passage of this bill [to grant a railroad right of way through Yellowstone National Park] is absolutely a commercial necessity...It is wholly an unattractive country. There is nothing whatever in it, no object of interest to the tourist, and there is not one out of twenty who ever visits for purposes of observation this remote section.

Mr. Cox [William R. Cox of North Carolina]: Mr. Chairman, I believe this bill is wrongly entitled. It should be denominated "A bill for the spoilation of this Yellowstone Park." This is a measure which is inspired by corporate greed and natural selfishness against national pride and natural beauty! It is a shame to despoil this park for mere mercenary purposes, such as running a railroad to these mines...

DEBATE IN THE UNITED STATES HOUSE OF REPRESENTATIVES, DECEMBER 14, 1886

Right top: Soda Butte in the Absaroka Mountains.
Bottom: Shoshone Lake, Yellowstone National Park.

stone Ecosystem has intensified, and it now appears that more is on the way. In 1984 I spoke of the potential for mining activity and mentioned several projects on the Shoshone National Forest east of the Yellowstone Park boundary, of a proposal for an operation at Jardine north of Mammoth, and of proposals in the Cooke City area.

The mine at Jardine is now on-line and producing. So too is a large operation on the north slope of the Absaroka-Beartooth Wilderness called the Stillwater Mining Company where paladium and platinum ore is produced. That ore will soon be processed at a new smelter that was originally proposed to be located near the Custer National Forest boundary but is now slated for construction about 35 miles to the north. In the same area, the New Jackpine Mine has been proposed near the headwaters of the East Boulder River. But the greatest concern of those who monitor mining in the ecosystem today are the massive proposed projects near Cooke City, Montana, barely beyond the boundaries of Yellowstone National Park.

During the last quarter of the 19th century and first two decades of the 20th century, Cooke City underwent a mining boom that produced substantial quantities of silver and gold. Mining activity here poisoned Soda Butte Creek with acid mine drainage for miles into Yellowstone National Park. At the time of this second edition, a proposed mining operation by Noranda Minerals and Crown Buttes Mines was in the planning stages. Called the "New World Project," this enormous operation is to be located just two miles south of Yellowstone Park in the Silver Gate–Cooke City area. As envisioned, the New World Project would produce a thousand tons of gold, silver and copper ore per day and come complete with mine, mill, tailings ponds, commuter traffic and a new 69,000-volt power line to run it

TOM MURPHY

PAT O'HARA

THREATENED AND ENDANGERED SPECIES: WHY SHOULD WE CARE?

At least 16 species of wildlife are considered to be rare, threatened, or in immediate danger of becoming extinct within the Greater Yellowstone Ecosystem. The area is home to four species of birds and mammals designated as threatened or endangered under the provisions of the Endangered Species Act of 1973. Threatened species are defined as those likely to become endangered in the foreseeable future, and include the grizzly bear and the bald eagle. Endangered species are those threatened with extinction throughout all or a significant portion of their range. In Yellowstone, the wolf and the peregrine falcon are listed as endangered.

With the possible exception of the wolf and the fisher (both of which may be extinct in Greater Yellowstone), these birds and animals still inhabit Yellowstone Park proper. But the fact that they exist doesn't mean that they find prime habitat there. Most of the wildlife species in the Yellowstone area once ranged far beyond, and are now compressed into an area that in terms of their historic range is small and does not provide optimum habitat. For bald and golden eagles, elk, grizzly bear, trumpeter swan, whooping crane, white pelican, bison, cougar and others, Yellowstone Park is too small; even the much larger Greater Yellowstone Ecosystem provides only marginal range. But it is now their only range, and for some of these creatures, the Greater Yellowstone area may be their last chance.

Why should we care? Why should we concern ourselves with the needs of a few uncommon birds and animals? What will be lost if they should pass into extinction? The answer to this last question is that we don't know what will be lost. Biologists of the U.S. Fish and Wildlife Service tell us in their publication, Endangered Means There's Still Time, that we are still largely ignorant of the complex ecological relationships that exist among living things in any given ecosystem. What we do know, however, tells us that each species occupies a special niche and fulfills a unique role in its ecosystem, presenting the potential of a chain reaction among all organisms with the loss of just one.

We also know that each species contains a reservoir of unique genetic material that has taken millions of years to evolve. For all of our genius, we have not yet learned to retrieve or re-create this genetic material, once lost.

Why should we care? We should care because the chemical secrets held in the earth's organisms have benefited people enormously and promise to benefit us even more in the years ahead. If a fungus known as Penicillium notatum had been wiped out, there would be no penicillin and perhaps none of the family of antibiotics that came in its wake. The exciting discovery that snails and mollusks are immune to cancer has triggered biological research in the hope that an understanding of this immunity can be applied to the prevention and cure of human cancers

There are other ways people will benefit by preserving the earth's life forms. Endangered species are environmental indicators, early (or perhaps late) warning systems that our management of the planet is not working well, that certain life forms simply can't live here any more, and that other species dependent upon those disappearing organisms are also in danger. Humans are not exempt from this threat—and neither will we be the last to go.

Then too, there are those who would argue for the protection of living organisms on the grounds that the widest possible range of diversity in plant and animal life simply makes our world a more interesting place.

In the entire 3,000 years before the arrival of whites in North America, fewer than a hundred species of birds and mammals (including such creatures as the mastodon and the sabre-tooth cat) became extinct. Yet in the 350 years since then, more than 500 species and subspecies of animals and plants have disappeared—an average of more than 140 species per century; and the trend toward extinction is accelerating almost beyond comprehension. Scientists estimate that today one species per day is disappearing from the earth. By the year 2000, that rate is projected to increase to one species per hour! At the turn of the century, a million species will likely have passed into extinction.

Should we care? If we do, for whatever reason, we must insist with all the vigor we can collectively command that the area in and around Yellowstone be protected against further encroachments upon the wildlife species that find their homes there.

all. It is difficult to see how the impacts of such a project can be mitigated to an acceptable level—acceptable at least to those who believe this area has values higher than those served by the short-term boom and bust cycle of hard rock mining.

Mining has a less concentrated impact on many other areas of Greater Yellowstone. But, from the claims in the Absaroka-Beartooth Wilderness on the north, to the gold lode near Pacific Creek in the Teton Wilderness on the south, the impact or potential impacts are the same: roads, drills, motor vehicles, heavy equipment, excavation, erosion and people, always more people.

WATER AND HYDROPOWER PROJECTS

The Greater Yellowstone area is one of North America's largest watersheds. In its mountains are found the headwaters of the Missouri River (including the Yellowstone, Madison, Gallatin, Clark's Fork of the Yellowstone, Shoshone and Grey Bull rivers), the Columbia River (including the Snake and Henrys Fork rivers), and the Green River.

For nearly a hundred years promoters and developers have had their eyes on Yellowstone's waters. As early as 1893 a serious scheme was put forth to utilize the waterfalls of Yellowstone National Park to generate electricity. In 1920 a plan to dam the Bechler Meadow in the southwest corner of the park was vigorously pursued, and that same year a dam was proposed for the Yellowstone River in Yankee Jim Canyon a few miles north of the park boundary. Every year between 1920 and 1924, Congress considered proposals to dam the Yellowstone River three miles below its outlet from Yellowstone Lake at Fishing Bridge; in 1926 a bill was introduced in Congress to omit the Bechler country in the southwest corner of the park from Yellow-

PAT O'HARA

stone so the Bechler River could be dammed; and in the early 1930s a plan was put forth to divert water from Yellowstone Lake to Shoshone Lake, then through tunnels into Idaho. In every instance congressional and public sentiment for the preservation of Yellowstone's rivers and lakes won out, but in some cases the forces for water projects were strong and the outcome was not secured easily.

Beyond the park boundary but well within the Greater Yellowstone Ecosystem, dams were built: on the Snake River at Jackson Hole, on the Henrys Fork at Island Park, on the Madison at Hebgen and Ennis lakes, and on a smaller scale at numerous locations. But today thousands of miles of waterways in the Greater Yellowstone Ecosystem continue as free-flowing, relatively natural rivers, streams and lakes. The Yellowstone River itself

remains undammed throughout its entire course from its headwaters above Yellowstone Lake in the Teton Wilderness to its confluence with the Missouri River near the Montana–North Dakota border. Many proposals have been put forth to dam the Yellowstone. By far the largest and most serious of these proposals is the one that would dam the Yellowstone River at Allen Spur 50 miles north of Yellowstone Park, just two miles above Livingston, Montana. Pursued at various times by federal agencies during the past several decades, the water impounded by a dam at Allen Spur would flood nearly the entire length of Montana's Paradise Valley.

A variety of hydropower and reclamation projects are proposed for the waters of the Greater Yellowstone Ecosystem. A look at one area, the

Henrys Fork River and its tributaries, just west of the Yellowstone Park boundary, illustrates the implications of such projects for the fish, wildlife, recreation and water quality of this part of the country.

In 1978 Congress passed the National Energy Act. One section of the act directed the Federal Energy Regulatory Commission (FERC) to formulate rules that would encourage small power production. In 1980 the agency required utility companies to purchase power generated by small producers at a favorable price. By providing a guaranteed market at a favorable price, much of the risk of hydropower development was removed. As a result, permit applications to tie up development sites for hydropower projects increased from 38 in 1979 to nearly 2,000 in 1981.

The Henrys Fork River is probably the finest stretch of fly fishing water in all of Idaho and is universally recognized as one of the world's premier trout fisheries. It is also home to 80 percent of the fragile tri-state trumpeter swan flock that depends heavily upon steady winter stream flows for ice-free winter habitat. On the Henrys Fork and its major tributaries today are a dozen or more proposed hydropower projects, all of which pose potential for significant fisheries damage through dewatering of streams, destruction of spawning areas, interruption of fish passage, and loss of fish to turbines. Additional aesthetic impacts, especially at some particularly scenic sites such as Upper and Lower Mesa Falls, also can be expected. Major projects proposed for the area include the installation of hydropower facilities at the

TOM MURPHY

Left: *Springtime on the east shore of Yellowstone Lake.*

Facing page: *Aerial view of the Cathedral Group, Grand Teton National Park.*

Island Park Dam, at Sheep Falls on the Henrys Fork River where application has been made for a permit and water rights, at three additional sites upstream of Sheep Falls, at both Upper and Lower Mesa Falls on the Henrys Fork, on the Warm River where the stream would be dewatered and diverted through a penstock and on the Falls River where a $10 million project east of Ashton, Idaho has been licensed.

No one knows what will come of the hydropower proposals for the Henrys Fork and its tributaries, but as in so many other instances in Greater Yellowstone today, the potential for development is there, and the rate at which it occurs will in all likelihood be based on economic rather than environmental considerations.

OTHER THREATS

While oil and gas development, geothermal energy, logging, mining, and water projects pose some of the largest threats to the Greater Yellowstone Ecosystem, myriad other activities and developments are underway that are less noticeable and of smaller scale, but are relentlessly chipping away at the environmental integrity of Greater Yellowstone.

Recreational resorts and subdivisions, many of which are located in prime lowland, riparian and wildlife winter-range areas, dot the landscape. Major ski areas at Teton Village near Jackson, Wyoming, Grand Targhee on the west slope of the Tetons, and Big Sky south of Bozeman, have had significant impacts in terms of the number of people they attract to the area as well as the physical impact of facility construction. Other resorts are planned.

At hundreds of other locations throughout Greater Yellowstone, large acreages are being

TOM MURPHY

subdivided and converted from open space to recreational second homes and condominiums as population spreads out and further encroaches onto the natural face of the ecosystem. The rate of such growth in some areas of Greater Yellowstone is simply staggering. In 1950, mostly agricultural Teton County, Wyoming, for example, had fewer than 2,600 residents. Today that number has increased by nearly 10 times and agriculture has declined steadily, now constituting only a small percentage of the local economy. The list is long: power lines, roads, poorly managed livestock operations that damage sensitive riparian areas and severely overtax the range—Greater Yellowstone can't accommodate it all and survive as the place we so value.

ADDITIONAL DANGERS

Other threats to the Greater Yellowstone Ecosystem are less subtle. Poaching of wildlife is a serious problem inside and outside Yellowstone Park. Grizzly bears and bighorn sheep bring thousands of dollars per animal on the illegal market, and a rack of elk antlers in velvet can fetch a hundred dollars per pound. Penalties for poaching are still pitifully low and law enforcement is expensive. The U.S. Fish and Wildlife Service has a few enforcement agents to cover an area twice the size of the Greater Yellowstone Ecosystem. And in Cooke City, a restaurant owner was deliberately feeding garbage to grizzly bears over an extended period virtually assuring the ultimate demise of the spoiled bears as they came into contact with people on their garbage forays. Severe and wide-spread damage to many public and private lands in the Greater Yellowstone area also is inflicted each year by careless drivers of off-road vehicles. Yet another threat to the ecosystem comes from outdoor enthusiasts who are visiting the back country in ever-larger numbers and are simply "loving it to death."

It doesn't make sense. Is it really in our long-term national interest to cut 10-inch-diameter trees that take 100 to 200 years to re-grow when those same trees can be grown in Georgia in 35 years profitably and without sacrificing major environmental values? We can't do everything here. We must decide what the Greater Yellowstone Ecosytem is best for; and based on that judgment, decide what's best for it.

At some future time, if we desire to do so, we can repeal the law [creating Yellowstone National Park] if it is in somebody's way.
SEN. LYMAN TRUMBALL,
SPEAKING ABOUT
LEGISLATION FOR THE
CREATION OF
YELLOWSTONE NATIONAL
PARK, 1872

PETE & ALICE BENGEYFIELD

Left: *Bison in the Hayden Valley, Yellowstone National Park.*

Facing page: *Morning fog from Mt. Washburn in the Absaroka Mountains.*

EPILOGUE

Since the first edition of this book was written in 1983, there have been significant changes in resource management philosophy in the Greater Yellowstone area.

During this eight-year period a remarkably widespread public awareness about Greater Yellowstone has developed. The term "Greater Yellowstone Ecosystem," virtually unheard of as recently as 1981, has become widely accepted and utilized by resource managers, the media, conservationists and political figures. The concept of a Greater Yellowstone Ecosystem has become legitimate, respectable, even fashionable. This new understanding represents a giant step toward protection of Greater Yellowstone, and the ecosystem concept has become an important focal point for the yet unresolved conflict over what must be done to protect the area and how best to accomplish it.

But while a new recognition of the concept of a Greater Yellowstone Ecosystem has developed, many of the policies and practices that this author discussed in the epilogue to the first edition have been slow to change. There has been no significant progress on national parks protection legislation or parkland acquisition; the politicization of the Department of the Interior and the National Park Service continues to impede sound resource management policies, and confusion among federal officials, politicians, and the American public generally about the purpose of national parks continues to prevail.

In the epilogues to the first and second editions of this book, I spoke of the debilitating effect that the policies of the Reagan administration and Reagan's Secretary of the Interior, James Watt, had had on the National Park Service, on attempts to create new national parks and expand existing parks, and on legislation that would provide greater protection the America's wildland heritage.

Watt and Reagan are gone now and the intensity of their anti-environmental rhetoric has gone with them. In their place we have the administration of George Bush, a self-described environmentalist who himself has spoken of the value of the Greater Yellowstone Ecosystem. This is promising, but the long and distressing list of developments, activities and policies that so threaten the Greater Yellowstone Ecosystem tend to overwhelm and discourage those who share concern about the future of the area, but efforts directed at wildland preservation in Greater Yellowstone are more vital today than at any time in the recent past. Not only is the magnitude of threats greater but, in many cases, they forebode deeper and longer-lasting impacts than earlier human activities in the area. In some cases, the damage they portend is simply irreversible.

Hopeful signs exist. A tide of conservation awareness is sweeping across America, and although it has not been translated into sufficient action, it is stirring powerfully. The president is taking note. Congress (local western delegations notwithstanding), where there has been a long history of bipartisan support for conservation, is taking a new interest in parks and wildlands generally and in Greater Yellowstone specifically. More and more, the American people realize that, as we finish the final years of the 20th century, we indeed are down to the last natural remnants of the earth.

There is also a dramatic new awareness among both federal resource managers and the public of the inestimable value of the Greater Yellowstone Ecosystem as a natural area, and of its fragility and susceptibility to disruption. This awareness is being translated into action by the determined and skilled efforts at the regional level by the Greater Yellowstone Coalition, at the local level by dozens of small, dedicated grass-roots organizations, and at the national level by America's most influential conservation organizations.

Beyond these beginnings, much remains to be done. In the end, what is needed is a mechanism for managing the ecosystem as an ecosystem, with decisions being based on sound biological grounds and area-wide considerations. This will not come easily. The inertia of old attitudes and special interests is powerful, and the issues are large and complex. It will not come at all unless we as a nation decide what is important to us in this area of the west and unless we commit ourselves to it. The choice is ours.

SELECTED BIBLIOGRAPHY

Agee, James K., and Darryll R. Johnson, eds. 1988. "Ecosystem Management for Parks and Wilderness," Workshop Synthesis, National Park Service Cooperative Park Studies Unit, Seattle, Contribution No. 62: pp. 1-39.

Agee, James K., and Darryll R. Johnson, eds. 1988. *Ecosystem Management for Parks and Wilderness,* University of Washington Press, Seattle.

Agee, James K., and Darryll R. Johnson, eds. 1989. "Ecosystem Management for National Parks," *Courier,* December 1989, pp. 6-9.

Bailey, R.G. 1976. *Ecoregions of the United States* [map], U.S. Forest Service, Intermountain Region, Ogden, Utah.

Barbee, Robert D. 1990. "Casting a Vote for Posterity," *Courier,* January 1990, pp. 12-13.

Barbee, Robert D., and John D. Varley. 1984. "The Paradox of Repeating Error: Yellowstone National Park from 1872 to Biosphere Reserve and Beyond," paper presented at the Conference for Managers of Biosphere Reserves, Great Smoky Mountains National Park, November 27-29.

Baur, Donald. 1987. "Special Focus Book Review on "Playing God in Yellowstone," *Land and Water Review,* 22(1), University of Wyoming College of Law, Laramie, Wyoming.

Brewer, Richard. 1979. *Principles of Ecology,* W.B. Saunders Company, Philadelphia.

Brewster, Wayne G. 1989. "Keeping the Cogs and Wheels: A Look at Ecosystem Management," *Courier,* December 1989, pp. 14-16.

Brewster, Wayne G. 1986. "Cogs and Wheels: Meditations on an Ecosystem," *Western Wildlands,* 12(3): pp. 7-11.

Camenzind, Franz J. 1985. "Yellowstone Ecosystem," *Park Science* 5(2): pp. 12-14.

Carr, Mary, and Sharon Eversman. 1991. *Roadside Ecology of Greater Yellowstone,* Mountain Press Publishing Co., Missoula, Montana.

Chase, Alston. 1986. *Playing God in Yellowstone: The Destruction of America's First National Park,* The Atlantic Monthly Press, Boston.

Clark, Tim. 1981. *Ecology of Jackson Hole Wyoming: A Primer,* T.W. Clark, Jackson, Wyoming.

Clark, Tim W., and Dusty Zaunbrecher. 1987. "The Greater Yellowstone Ecosystem: The Ecosystem Concept in Natural Resource Policy and Management," *Renewable Resources Journal,* Summer 1987, pp. 8-19.

Clark, Tim W. 1989. *Rare, Sensitive and Threatened Species of the Greater Yellowstone Ecosystem,* Northern Rockies Conservation Cooperative, Jackson, Wyoming.

Clark, Tim W., and Ann H. Harvey. 1988. *Management of the Greater Yellowstone Ecosystem: An Annotated Bibliography,* Northern Rockies Conservation Cooperative, Jackson, Wyoming.

Corn, M. Lynne, Ross Gorte, and George Siehl. 1985. *Issues Surrounding the Greater Yellowstone Ecosystem: A Brief Review.* Congressional Research Service, The Library of Congress, October 17, 1985, pp. 337-372 in U.S. House Committee on Interior and Insular Affairs, "Greater Yellowstone Ecosystem: Oversight Hearing," 99th Cong., 1st sess., October 24, 1985.

Corn, M. Lynne, and Ross W. Gorte. 1986. *Yellowstone: Ecosystem, Resources, and Management,* Congressional Research Service, The Library of Congress, December 12, 1986.

Craighead, Frank. 1979. *Track of the Grizzly,* Sierra Club Books, San Francisco.

Despain, Don, Douglas Houston, Mary Meagher, and Paul Schullery. 1986. *Wildlife in Transition: Man and Nature on Yellowstone's Northern Range,* Roberts Rinehart, Boulder, Colorado.

Fishbien, Seymour. 1989. *Yellowstone Country: The Enduring Wonder,* National Geographic Society, Washington, D.C.

Franklin, K.E. 1986. "The Process at Work: Greater Yellowstone," *American Forests* 92 (October): pp. 22-27, 53-55.

Galbraith, Alan F. 1986. "Headwaters of the West: The Yellowstone Ecosystem." *Western Wildlands,* 12(3): pp. 12-13.

Glick, Dennis, Mary Carr, and Robert Ekey, eds. 1991. *Environmental Profile of the Greater Yellowstone Ecosystem.* Greater Yellowstone Coalition, Bozeman, Montana.

Greater Yellowstone Coalition. 1986. *Greater Yellowstone Challenges 1986: An Inventory of Management Issues and Development Projects in the Greater Yellowstone Ecosystem,* Greater Yellowstone Coalition, Bozeman, Montana.

Greater Yellowstone Coalition. 1986. *A Model for Information Integration and Management for the Centennial Ecosystem,* Greater Yellowstone Coalition, Bozeman, Montana.

Greater Yellowstone Coordinating Committee. 1987. *The Greater Yellowstone Area: An Aggregation of National Park and National Forest Management Plans,* U.S. Forest Service, Intermountain Region, Ogden, Utah.

Greater Yellowstone Coordinating Committee. 1990. "Vision for the Future, A Framework for Coordination in the Greater Yellowstone Area" (draft), U.S. Forest Service/National Park Service, Billings, Montana.

Gruell, George. 1986. "The Importance of Fire in the Greater Yellowstone Ecosystem," *Western Wildlands,* 12(3): pp. 14-18.

Harvey, A.H. 1987. "Interagency Conflict and Coordination in Wildlife Management: A Case Study," master's thesis, University of Michigan.

Hocker, P.M. 1979. "Yellowstone: The Region Is Greater than the Sum of Its Parks," *Sierra,* 64(4): pp. 8-12.

Houston, D.B. 1968. "The Shiras Moose in Jackson Hole, Wyoming," *Grand Teton Natural History Association Technical Bulletin,* Number 1, GTNHA, Moose, Wyoming.

Houston, Douglas B. 1971. "Ecosystems of National Parks," *Science,* 172: pp. 648-651.

Hunter, Malcolm L., Jr. 1990. *Wildlife, Forests, and Forestry: Principles of Managing Forests for Biological Diversity,* Prentice-Hall, Englewood Cliffs, New Jersey.

Jones, C.E. 1988. *The Conservation of Ecosystems and Species,* Chapman and Hall, New York.

Keefer, William R. 1987. *The Geologic Story of Yellowstone National Park,* Geological Survey Bulletin #1347, reprinted by Yellowstone Library and Museum Association, Mammoth, Wyoming.

Koshland, D.E., Jr. 1987. "Inexorable Laws and the Ecosystem," *Science,* 237 (4810): p. 9.

Kuchler, A.W. 1964. "Potential Natural Vegetation of the Coterminus United States," American Geographical Society, New York.

Leopold, A. S., S.A. Cain, C. M. Cottam, I.N. Gabrielson, and T. L. Kimball. 1963. *Wildlife Management in the National Parks,* Report of the Advisory Board on Wildlife Management to Secretary of Interior Udall, March 4, 1963, U.S. Government Printing Office, Washington, D.C.

Little, Charles E. 1987. "The Challenge of Greater Yellowstone," *Wilderness* 51(179): pp. 18-56.

Mattson, David J., and Daniel P. Reinhart. 1987. *Grizzly Bear, Red Squirrels, and Whitebark Pine: Third Year Progress Report.* Report to the Interagency Grizzly Bear Study Team, Bozeman, Montana.

McNamee, T. 1985. Statement to the Subcommittee on Public Lands and National Parks of the Committee on Interior and Insular Affairs, U.S. House of Representatives, October 24, 1985.

McNamee, Thomas. 1984. *The Grizzly Bear,* Alfred A. Knopf, New York.

Mott, William Penn. 1985. Speech before the Greater Yellowstone Coalition Annual Meeting, Lake Hotel, Yellowstone National Park, Wyoming, June 8, 1985.

National Academy of Sciences. 1963. *A Report by the Advisory Committee to the National Park Service on Research of the National Academy of Sciences-National Research Council* (Robins Report), National Academy of Sciences–National Research Council, Washington, D.C.

National Parks and Conservation Association. 1989. *National Parks: From Vignettes to a Global View,* National Parks and Conservation Association, Washington, D.C.

National Park Service. 1980. *State of the Parks Report,* NPS Office of Science and Technology, Washington.

National Park Service. 1990. *Wolves for Yellowstone? A Report to Congress,* Volume II: Research and Analysis, National Park Service, Washington, D.C.

National Park Service. 1986. "A Detailed Response from the National Park Service to 'The Grizzly and the Juggernaut'," Yellowstone National Park, Wyoming.

Newmark, William D. 1985. "Legal and Biotic Boundaries of Western North American National Parks: A Problem of Congruence," *Biological Conservation* 33: pp. 197-208.

Norse, Elliott A., Kenneth L. Rosenbaum, David S. Wilcove, Bruce A. Wilcox, William H. Romme, David W. Johnston, and Martha L. Stout. 1986. "Maintaining Biological Diversity in Large Wildlands: The Greater Yellowstone Ecosystem," *Conserving Biological Diversity in Our National Forests,* The Wilderness Society, pp. 91-106.

Peek, J.M. 1980. "Natural Regulation of Ungulates (What Constitutes a Real Wilderness?)," *Wildlife Society Bulletin* 8: pp. 217-27.

Penn, Bradley G. 1986. "Multiple Use in the Yellowstone Ecosystem: Oil and Gas Exploration." *Western Wildlands,* 12(3): pp. 24-26.

Pimato, Dawn, and Don Whittemore. 1989. *Status Report on the Yellowstone Grizzly Bear,* Greater Yellowstone Coalition, Bozeman, Montana.

Reed, Nathaniel P. 1989. *From Wild Trout to Wild Ecosystems,* Address to Wild Trout IV Conference, Sept. 18-19, 1989, Yellowstone National Park.

Reese, Rick. 1984. *Greater Yellowstone: The National Park and Adjacent Wildlands,* American Geographic Publishing, Helena, Montana.

Reese, Rick. 1984. "Observations and Impressions of the Recent Meeting in Cody," Memorandum to Parties Concerned with Fishing Bridge Issue, August 16, 1984, Greater Yellowstone Coalition, Bozeman, Montana.

Robbins, Jim. 1984. "Coalition Says Yellowstone Needs Elbow Room," *New York Times,* October 21, p. 29A.

Rolston, Holmes. 1990. "Biology and Philosophy in Yellowstone," *Biology and Philosophy,* 5: pp. 241-258.

Rolston, Holmes. 1986. "Can and Ought We to Follow Nature?", *Philosophy Gone Wild,* Prometheus Books, Buffalo, New York.

Schullery, Paul. 1980. *The Bears of Yellowstone,* Yellowstone Library and Museum Association, Mammoth, Wyoming.

Schullery, Paul. 1988. *Mountain Time,* Simon and Schuster, New York.

Sierra Club. 1986. *Yellowstone Under Siege: Oil and Gas Leasing in the Greater Yellowstone Region,* Sierra Club, San Francisco.

Streubel, Donald. 1989. *Small Mammals of the Greater Yellowstone Ecosystem,* Roberts Rinehart, Boulder, Colorado.

The Wilderness Society. 1987. "The Greater Yellowstone Ecosystem," *Forests of the Future: An Assessment of the National Forest Planning Process,* Washington, D.C., pp. 50-55.

The Wilderness Society. 1987. *Management Directions for the National Forests of the Greater Yellowstone Ecosystem,* The Wilderness Society, Washington, D.C.

Tixier, J.S. 1986. "The Greater Yellowstone: An Introduction to an Area and Its Issues," *Western Wildlands,* 12(3): pp. 2-6.

Waring, R.H. and W.H. Schlesinger. 1985. *Forest Ecosystems: Concepts and Management,* Academic Press, Inc., New York.

Weaver, J.L. 1978. "The Wolves of Yellowstone," National Park Service Report, Number 14, Washington, D.C.

Weaver, John. 1986. "Of Wolves and Grizzly Bears," *Western Wildlands,* 12(3): pp. 27-29.

Wuerthner, George. 1988. *Yellowstone and the Fires of Change,* Haggis House, Salt Lake City.

INDEX

HENRY H. HOLDSWORTH

A runoff stream from Upper Geyser Basin offers warmth in winter.